Rewire Your Brain for LOVE

Praise for *Rewire Your Brain for Love*

"This is great stuff. The latest, best mindful brain science in a wildly practical form, with wise and clear practices that can radically transform your relationships."

— **Jack Kornfield, PhD**, author of *The Wise Heart: A Guide to the Universal Teachings of Buddhist Psychology*

"Change your brain's pathways and you change the path of your relationships: that's what neuropsychologist and psychotherapist Marsha Lucas, PhD, offers in ***Rewire Your Brain for Love****. She uses her sense of humor and compassion as much as her knowledge of neuroscience and mindfulness to get you growing toward new, more vibrant relationships. Incredibly useful and highly engaging!"*

— **Marci Shimoff**, *New York Times* best-selling author of *Happy for No Reason* and *Love for No Reason*

*"****Rewire Your Brain for Love*** *is delightfully engaging and easy to read. Everyone will find something life-enhancing inside these pages."*

— **Christiane Northrup, MD, OB/GYN** physician and author of the *New York Times* bestsellers *Women's Bodies, Women's Wisdom* and *The Wisdom of Menopause*

"Honest, warmhearted, and funny. Lucas explains neuroscience in plain English, so all of us can understand. She brings great clarity to the sometimes murky waters of romantic relationships and gives us a wonderful introduction to mindfulness meditation and its benefits."

— **Sharon Salzberg**, author of *Real Happiness*

"Marsha Lucas takes the mystery out of two mysterious subjects—the inner workings of our brains and the successful pursuit of true love. She's a wise and funny cupid, bringing together our hearts and minds as she explains amygdalas and anxiety, frontal lobes and commitment-phobes. She's an excellent advocate for meditation, presenting its benefits in a unique, compelling way."

— **Priscilla Warner**, *New York Times* bestseller and author of *Learning to Breathe*

"Each of us has the potential to live with an open, loving heart. This book shows us how meditation awakens our capacity for increased presence, intimacy, and understanding in our relationships. With clarity and humor, Marsha Lucas gives us both the fascinating science behind this transformation, and the practices that make it possible."

— **Tara Brach, PhD**, author of *Radical Acceptance* and founder of the Insight Meditation Community of Washington

*"With **Rewire Your Brain for Love**, Marsha Lucas has pulled off an achievement that is as valuable as it is rare: she synthesizes complex neurophysiological information about the brain's role in relationships, in clear, reader-friendly ways; and combines this with really smart, practical, effective tools and suggestions for beefing up the capacity for attachment, drawing from a very smart, sophisticated combination of meditative, mind-body, and cognitive-behavioral techniques. And there's a bonus: she's a really fine, witty, accessible writer. Anyone who struggles with garden-variety anxiety about love, all the way up to full-blown phobia, should read this book, more than once. And it should be dog-eared and well worn on every therapist's reference shelf."*

— **Belleruth Naparstek, LISW**, author of *Invisible Heroes* and creator of the Health Journeys guided-imagery series

"Dr. Lucas shows readers how to use the power of neuroplasticity—the capacity of the mind to change the brain—to build up the 'circuits' of resilience, empathy, and assertiveness for relationships. Her voice is warm, funny, down-to-earth, practical, and so very helpful. This book is like having a best friend who is both savvy about the brain and a world-class therapist."

— **Rick Hanson, PhD**, author of *Buddha's Brain*

"With entertaining humor and enlightening clarity, Dr. Lucas blends cutting-edge discoveries in neurobiology and psychology with time-honored practices from ancient wisdom traditions to help us navigate the challenges of intimate relationships. Full of real-life examples and practical tools, this book is a delightful must-read for anyone wanting to get along better with other people."

— **Ronald D. Siegel, PsyD**, Assistant Clinical Professor of Psychology, Harvard Medical School; author of *The Mindfulness Solution*

*"Marsha Lucas's **Rewire Your Brain for Love** is a smart and reader-friendly guide for an exciting journey through our hearts and brains. Dr. Lucas skillfully interweaves her therapeutic and neuroscientific knowledge with personal wisdom into a rich, meaningful, and accessible tapestry that expands our self-awareness in the service of sustaining and deepening our relationships."*

— **Louis Cozolino, PhD**, professor of Psychology, Pepperdine University; author of *The Neuroscience of Human Relationships*

"This book is a fun and funky ride into love and neuroscience. You will learn, laugh and maybe change how your brain deals with the most important moments in your love life."

— **Dr. Sue Johnson**, author of *Hold Me Tight: Seven Conversations for a Lifetime of Love*

"Marsha Lucas, PhD, provides an accessible and practical guide to help us bring alive the exciting intersection of mindfulness and neuroscience for healthier relationships and a better life."

— **Elisha Goldstein**, author of *The Now Effect* and co-author of *A Mindfulness-Based Stress Reduction Workbook*

"Ever wondered why you get stuck in the same old relationship patterns? With no-nonsense wit and warmth, Marsha Lucas shows you what's happening at brain level when habits form, persist, and most importantly, shift. Crucially, she also shows you how to apply this knowledge to transform your intimate connections—all with the simple practice of mindfulness. This book will bring joy not just to many readers, but to those who share their lives."

— **Ed Halliwell**, co-author of *The Mindful Manifesto*

"You hold in your hands a unique piece of work. Marsha guides you carefully, to help you understand the unique benefits of mindfulness from the inside out, and so helps to ignite or re-ignite your passion for the meditative practice. Better relationships lie at the heart of a life of health and well-being. Through reading this book, you learn to become an electrician of your own brain, and discover specific mind techniques that lead to a better relationship with both yourself and those close to you. A delight to read—highly recommended!"

— **Shamash Alidina**, author of *Mindfulness for Dummies* and *Relaxation for Dummies*

"Psych Central's Recommendation: Worth Your Time! ***Rewire Your Brain for Love*** *is one of those great hybrids between self-help and education. If you're looking for a method to tackle relationship problems (or even just 'life' problems), you'd be hard-pressed to find a better primer."*

— **Dan Berkowitz**, PsychCentral Book Reviews

*"****Rewire Your Brain for Love*** *. . . successfully combines mindfulness, psychotherapy, and neuroscience to illustrate how retraining one's brain leads to better relationships. Whereas many self-help books focus on improving romantic partnerships, this book refreshingly aims to benefit one's relationship with oneself and everyone else, including lovers."*

— **Jill Allen**, *ForeWord Magazine*

"We live in a world of failed relationships and loss of love. Dr. Lucas has given us the science and clinical application of mindfulness meditation tools to help us heal ourselves, our relationships, and our world. We are all in need of this sage advice."

— **Allan Warshowsky, MD, FACOG, ABIHM,** Director Emeritus of the American Board of Integrative Holistic Medicine

"This excellent book takes the reader on an exciting journey of self discovery and healing through the emerging field of neurobiology and mindfulness meditation. Dr. Lucas presents scientific concepts in an easily understood manner and goes on to assist the reader to learn meditation techniques that have demonstrated proven healing benefits for emotional, psychological, and physical problems as well as for those individuals who strive for optimal wellness. This book is a must-read for everyone."

— **Leonard A. Wisneski, MD, FACP,** professor at George Washington University, Georgetown University, University of Colorado; author of *The Scientific Basis of Integrative Medicine*

"I highly recommend this book for anyone who is interested in improving their relationships, in gaining insight into their behaviors, and in exploring meditation practices. Dr. Lucas presents the information in her book in a friendly, loving, and honest way that gives a wonderful overview of the inner workings of our brains and an easy introduction into the world of mindfulness."

— **Sandra E. James,** reviewer, *Mindfulness* journal

*"**Rewire Your Brain for Love** is a must-have for anyone wanting to improve their emotional and relationship health. Though a book could never be the 'be-all-end-all' and guarantee your relationship dreams come true, it can surely provide you with guideposts and tools to give yourself a great starting point. This one packs a powerful, research-backed punch. Don't miss it."*

— **Lisa Brookes Kift, MFT**

Rewire Your Brain for LOVE

Creating Vibrant Relationships Using the Science of Mindfulness

Marsha Lucas, PhD

HAY HOUSE

Hay House Publishers India

Australia • India

United Kingdom • United States

Hay House Publishers (India) Pvt. Ltd.
Muskaan Complex, Plot No.3, B-2 Vasant Kunj, New Delhi-110 070, India
Hay House Inc., PO Box 5100, Carlsbad, CA 92018-5100, USA
Hay House UK, Ltd., The Sixth Floor, Watson House, 54 Baker Street, W1U 7BU, UK
Hay House Australia Pty Ltd., 18/36 Ralph St., Alexandria NSW 2015, Australia

Email: contact@hayhouse.co.in
www.hayhouse.co.in

First Indian edition 2022

Cover design: Julie Davison • *Interior design:* Tricia Breidenthal

FOR SALE IN THE INDIAN SUBCONTINENT AND THE MIDDLE EAST ONLY

ISBN 978-93-91067-94-6

Printed at Repro India Limited

For Duncan and Gabriel
and everyone who aspires to be
part of a more empathic world

CONTENTS

INTRODUCTION

Rewiring Your Brain for Love

The Best Do-It-Yourself Project You'll Ever Do

We live in a culture that holds tantalizing promise for a satisfying life with good friends and good relationships, yet the rate of depression, stress, overwork, and divorce—or simply choosing to veg out with the TV or Internet every night, instead of having real, satisfying relationships with real people—has literally reached pandemic proportions.

We're bombarded with helpful hints from relationship gurus on television and in magazines who promise they have the secret set of words and behaviors to make you happy: "simply follow these five simple rules!"

But you have (repeatedly) tried what they've suggested and you still aren't happy—and your relationships still don't cut it.

The pharmaceutical companies advertise to millions about curing depression and social anxiety with a little pill once a day. And yet the majority of people still suffer in their search for better relationships and more satisfying lives.

What's going on?

To answer this question, we turn to neuroscience: the way your brain is wired can either help you have happy, satisfying relationships or it can be a huge obstacle to healthy love.

So where does this wiring come from? Unfortunately, most of your brain's wiring for relationships was determined unbelievably early in your brain's development—before you were about two years old. (Your interactions as a baby have an enormous, lifelong influence on how your brain does relationships.)

The good news, though, is that you can rewire your brain for better relationships. You can change your old "relationship brain" neural pathways and develop new and improved ones using simple, 2,500-year-old mind-training techniques that are more precise than a neurosurgeon's blade, and without all the mess. The ancient practice of mindfulness meditation, as it turns out, produces real, measurable changes in the brain in key places so that deeper connections, better love, and healthier relationships can really take hold.

In as little as 20 minutes a day.

Whaddaya think? Are your relationships worth 20 minutes a day?

Open Mind + Well-Wired Brain = New Frontiers

Something to let you know up front: I get excited by neuroscience. A little strange, I know, but it'll come in extremely handy as we go along. My hope is that you'll get a little excited by it, too, once you realize what a powerful tool it is.

As recently as ten years ago, neuroscience maintained an ironclad rule about neurons in the brain: once you reached adulthood, you couldn't grow any new brain cells—they only died off as the years went on. (Of course, you could accelerate the process of neuronal die-off, depending on what kind of damage you were doing through drug use, head injury, and so on.) This "rule" also meant that old connections within the brain—those neuronal pathways that determine how you react—couldn't be replaced if they were damaged. It was all downhill after the brain "completed" its development at the golden age of 25. Yikes.

Well, we found out pretty recently that that idea is wrong. Really wrong. We can, in fact, not only cause the neurons in our brains to change and to grow new connections and pathways, but we can produce *new* neurons, throughout our entire lives. It's called *neuroplasticity,* and it's the most radical finding in neuroscience since, well, the discovery that the brain wasn't just a cooling device for the body. (I'm not kidding: that idea goes back as far as the ancient Egyptians and went largely unchallenged for millennia.)

What does this mean for you and your relationships? If you can grow new connections and new neurons, your old, getting-in-your-way wiring can be redirected and/or overridden. *You can rebuild it.*

As a psychologist who has been working with patients for over 20 years, I find that radically exciting.

So how exactly do you change those structures and connections into supporters of happy relationships? Recent studies by leading neuroscientists and biobehaviorists—researchers from Harvard, UCLA, MIT, Princeton, Stanford, and Cambridge, to name a few—have shown that mindfulness practice promotes changes in your brain in areas and ways that promote healthier relationships with yourself and others.

The neurological changes seen in the brains of mindfulness meditators show up in how they feel, how they deal with their feelings, and how they do relationships. And it doesn't take years of practice—many beneficial effects are seen in the earliest stages of practice, in as little as a few weeks of practicing 20 minutes a day.

Can't do 20 minutes? That's perfectly okay; start with two.

Think you just can't do it at all?

About 95 percent of my patients thought the same thing. And nearly all of them found out that they could meditate—and much more easily than they thought, once they tried it with the kinds of knowledge and simple instruction you'll find in this book.

You don't have to become a monk or a vegetarian or spend hours contemplating your navel. You don't need to hum "Om" over and over, trying to get your brain to be still or empty.

What you do during mindfulness meditation is practice simply noticing your mind's busyness (a.k.a. your thoughts and feelings) and not getting all tangled up in it. You don't even have to sit while you do it (and you definitely don't have to sit like a pretzel). You can do walking meditation, eating meditation, lying-down meditation, or even washing-dishes meditation. With practice, you can meditate anywhere, during just about any activity.

I've been practicing psychotherapy for over 20 years, and I have always been deeply honored to help people as they dig in and do the often difficult work of creating better lives for themselves. I resisted becoming a physician/psychiatrist/neurologist because I knew early on that medication was not the only path to well-being. Since I began using mindfulness meditation with my patients, I have been privileged to witness some of the most amazing shifts and improvements. It has been the single most remarkable "ingredient" in therapy I've ever seen. We've known for a while from research that the most reliable predictive factor in psychotherapy outcome is the patient's sense of an authentic, attuned relationship with the therapist.[1] I believe that by adding mindfulness meditation, we're adding another authentic, attuned relationship for patients—the one *within themselves.*

By using simple mindfulness meditation, you can rewire your brain's relationship pathways—and change your life.

This book is about why and how to use mindfulness meditation as a simple, good-for-you approach to rewiring your brain for better, healthier, juicier romantic relationships.

The Seven "High-Voltage" Benefits

Consider this: developmental psychologists talk about essential characteristics that are seen in people with healthy, attuned childhood relationships—characteristics that bode incredibly well for these people's ability to have healthy relationships in adulthood.

And then this: *those same characteristics are seen in people who practice mindfulness*—plus bonus characteristics.

To top it all off: the latest scientific research has increasingly been showing that these characteristics are associated with areas of the brain that change as a result of mindfulness.

As I've worked with my patients and consulted with other psychotherapists, I've found that the most helpful way to think about these characteristics is to group them into a list of seven acquirable skills. These are skills you can develop and grow within yourself, within your brain—and they seem to be the most powerful in creating and sustaining a healthy and happy relationship:

1. *Management of your body's reactions*
2. *Regulation of your response to fear*
3. *Emotional resilience*
4. *Response flexibility*
5. *Insight (self-knowing)*
6. *Empathy and attunement—within yourself and with others*
7. *Perspective shift from "me" to "we"*

In the work I do with my patients, I've seen that the growth of these seven characteristics has such an important impact on interactions with others that I call them the "high-voltage" relationship benefits. We'll be exploring each of these in Part II of the book.

Daniel Siegel, MD, a Harvard-trained psychiatrist and an expert on childhood attachment was the person who first made me aware of the connection between these documented and compelling characteristics of well-being, seen in people who grew up with healthy, attuned attachments, and the brain structures and pathways shown to change with mindfulness practice. Since then, I've been seeing the results confirmed through my psychology practice, in myself, and in the lives of my friends and colleagues. I want you to benefit as well.

The Wiring Diagram of This Book

I've written this book in three parts. In each one, I'll teach you, in accessible, helpful ways, why your brain works the way it does when it comes to connections with others—and you'll get the information and tools to break free of old patterns and move into healthier, more vibrant relationships.

In Part I of the book ("Understanding Your Current Wiring Diagram: Please Read the Owner's Manual *Before* Attempting Repairs"), you'll learn first about how your brain got into the tough spot it's in—how your earliest experiences with love, attachment, and relationships wired your brain for "how to do love."

Once you know more about how you got your current wiring, I'll help you get familiar with some very basic neuroanatomy. (Don't panic! I've road-tested this brain lesson on scores of people whose eyes would typically glaze over at the first utterance of the word *neuroanatomy,* and they've all been happy to find out that it's not hard—or boring—after all.) It's important to know some basics about the brain's structure and connections in the way they affect relationships. That way, you can really understand what and where the miswirings are, how they play out in your relationship struggles, and what your new wiring plan needs to look like. I've seen time and again how much easier this little bit of knowledge makes it to let go of old, unhelpful ways of thinking about yourself and the relationship problems you've been trying to solve.

Part II ("Becoming Your Own Master Electrician: Essential Relationship Wiring Features and How to Power Them Up") is where you'll roll up your sleeves and get wiring. And because I want you to get real, lasting benefits from what I've learned and written in the pages that follow, I strongly recommend that you start with Chapter 1 and experience the book in order. I know it might be tempting to pick and choose the chapters that you want to read (and the ones you want to skip—or avoid), but the trek will yield much more benefit if you approach it one step at a time.

I've structured the book so that the benefits you gain through these practices work in a progression—each benefit is supported by the ones that come before it, and the ones that come later in the list keep the earlier ones strong. Like building a house, it works better if you start with the foundation and methodically work your way up. The chapters in Part II move from the bottom of your brain's wiring to the top—from your relationship with yourself toward your relationships with others.

For example, becoming better at being aware of and regulating your body's responses to the world "out there," which is where Part II begins, gives you the foundation for what's next: getting a handle on the most relationship-derailing emotion of all—*fear.* Once fear isn't shorting out your relationship brain, you're ready to rock 'n' roll with increased resilience with all of your other emotions . . . which then affords you more room to choose from a wider range of healthier responses . . . and so on, through all of the high-voltage benefits.

At the end of each chapter in Part II (and at the end of Part III) is a mindfulness meditation/exercise. It'll probably serve you best to practice the meditation at the end of each chapter at least a few times before moving on to the next chapter. Along the way, you'll undoubtedly find some meditation practices that you like better than others—great! Feel free to bookmark those and return to them any time you want, but also be sure to keep moving forward and trying the ones that come next.

What do I mean by "practice"? I mean some meditating on a regular basis for a reasonable amount of time. The regular basis that's most helpful for most people is once a day; if you want to practice twice a day, go for it. As for what constitutes a reasonable amount of time, I recommend that you set aside 20 minutes to practice a given meditation. Longer is great, but not necessary. I'll say it over and over, though—if you can't do 20 minutes, start with two. As a wise dental hygienist once told me, "Flossing once a week is better than not flossing at all." The same goes for meditating.

You'll also find some other exercises in the book that are helpful additions to the meditations. I invite you to at least try them and see if you find them useful.

All of that said, this is your book and, more important, your journey! I definitely understand about wanting to do it your own way or resisting a prescription (it's my own first reflex in many situations). If you find yourself bumping up against some internal push-back—which might look like forgetting to meditate, skipping past a "useless" chapter, or losing the book—I invite you to take a little time to gently but persistently poke around at it: *Why might I be tempted to push back right here?* or *Why was it that when I got to this particular point in my progress, I started to lose my traction?*

In Part III ("You've Got the Power"), I'll guide you through the maintenance of your new and improved wiring and how to handle obstacles that might come up as you live more fully in your brain and your relationships. I'll also direct you to resources for learning more and getting support, including articles, books, and web-based resources.

Many of the people I've worked with said that they always knew meditation might be good for them, but either they never got around to trying it, or they practiced but never felt anything more than some healthy relaxation. After I worked with them for a while, though, they learned the things that you will know after reading this book—and they understood that meditation really could be beneficial. They understood what meditation was doing in tangible ways to change their brains—and to change their love lives. The vast majority of them found not only that it was more compelling to practice regularly, but that it was more helpful than they'd ever expected or experienced before.

Sara Lazar, PhD, a Harvard neuroscientist who studies the effects of mindfulness meditation on the brain, has said, "The thing that surprised me most about this research is how many senior practitioners and meditation teachers say that it motivates them to practice during the times when their meditation seems to be going nowhere." Meditators, she says, often tell her, "I used to think that I was wasting my time because my mind was all over the place. This helps to keep me on the cushion because I remember how significant these changes are."[2] I've had the same experience myself—I was a meditation giver-upper until I discovered the neuroscience connection. When I hear similar reports from my patients, I'm thrilled.

As with anything worthwhile, rewiring your brain with mindfulness meditation takes practice and commitment. But the payoff, as you will see, is well worth the effort. One of the preeminent researchers in this field, Richard Davidson, PhD, has said that using mindfulness meditation to shift your brain's emotional set point isn't something that takes years—big benefits come at the beginning of practice. My deepest wish is for you to give this gift to yourself, and I've written this book to help you get there.

Well, I'm guessing that you're eager (and maybe a little anxious) to get going. If you and I were sitting together, I'd probably look at you warmly, smile, take a breath, and say something like, "Take a breath." (Profound, I know.) The next thing I'd say would be something like this: "You've decided to go on this mountain trek. It's your trek, and you're the expert about your mountain—even if you don't know that yet. Think of me as a sherpa, one of those experienced Himalayan guides. While I've never explored *your* particular mountain, I have years of experience guiding people on their many and varied mountains. I also have some of the best tools and techniques to show you, and last but not least, I have the authentic and sincere desire to help you."

Ultimately, it's your journey. If you're ready, let's go.

PART I

Understanding Your Current Wiring Diagram

Please Read the Owner's Manual *Before* Attempting Repairs

CHAPTER 1

Early Relationship Experiences

Attached at the ~~Hip~~ Hippocampus

When I was a kid, my mother tried to limit what I watched on TV, which now, as a parent myself, I appreciate. But there were shows she'd censor that made no sense—like *Marcus Welby, MD,* about a wise old family physician with a kindly bedside manner. To this day, I have no idea why she was so worried about such a benign TV show—except that my mother worried about everything, and what torqued her the most were relationships, including the one with me.

Her anxiety around being connected emotionally influenced the way my brain became wired for relationships far more than any TV show I could have watched.

And that's the bottom line.

Your first experiences with relationships—those you have with your parents—have a huge influence on how you deal with relationships throughout your life. The your-parents-to-you relationship covertly operates in important, behind-the-scenes ways in your later you-to-your-partner romantic relationships. The lessons of our primary childhood relationships run so deep and so strong—and often *waaaaay* outside our conscious awareness—that we all find it extraordinarily challenging to overcome them.

Louis Cozolino, PhD, is a clinical psychologist who studies and writes about neuroscience, especially about how our brains influence our relationships (and vice versa), and I appreciate his clear take on this: "Because the first few years of life are a period of exuberant brain development, early experiences have a disproportionate impact on the shaping of our neural systems, with lifelong consequences."[1] The accumulated experiences of your relationship with your parents is like a powerful computer program that's always running in the background in your brain, but the difference is that the "uninstall" feature is impossible to find.

This program—how it goes between our parents and us, and what we learn about relationships from them in early childhood—is, in psych-speak, *attachment*. For the vast majority of people, attachment styles fall into two broad categories: *secure* and *insecure*.

Slightly more than half of adults in the US (55 percent), according to research, fall into the "healthy" category, called a *secure* attachment style.[2] Our parents were able to regularly tune in to us, meeting our emotional needs on a consistent basis and giving us a sense of safety, security, and well-being. (Some of those 55-percenters may have what's called "earned" secure attachment, through experiences after childhood—such as we're working on in this book.)

But that means, of course, that the other 45 percent of us didn't have a consistent, responsive secure-attachment harbor. As a result, we have an *insecure* style of attachment. We tend to have either an ambivalent/anxious feeling about seeking comfort or closeness (we want it, but we perceive it as risky) or a desire to minimize or avoid relationships altogether. We develop this style as the best adaptation to our environment, in the same way that people who live in subarctic regions adapt by eating large quantities of fatty foods to produce extra body heat, wearing heavy clothing, and sleeping in a huddle.

Why is knowing about early attachment so important?

Because the style of attachment we develop in childhood is most often a lifetime deal. It drives and influences how we interact with others and how we see ourselves in relationships, and, as much as we might not like to believe this, it deeply influences the kinds of partners we attract and are attracted to. All too often, they end up being precisely what we *don't* need, despite our best efforts.

It Isn't about Dickens

When I explain all of this to my patients, I almost invariably hear something like, "Don't you think this is a bit over the top? Okay, based on how you look at it, I probably fall into the insecure category, but it's not like my childhood was something out of *Oliver Twist.*"

I'm not talking about traumatic, awful childhoods and horrific, evil parents. And I'm definitely not jumping on top of the pile of mother-blamers and father-bashers who hold their parents responsible for everything that subsequently doesn't go well in their own lives. But the fact is that, fairly often, ordinary, run-of-the-mill parent-child attachment simply falls short of what we need to create healthy, secure relationships later in our lives. (My husband and I have often thought about keeping a logbook of all of the times we mess up as parents, and then simply handing it to our kids when they're grown, saying, "Here, this'll give your therapist a head start.")

Having an insecure attachment style isn't the equivalent of being broken, deranged, wacko, or some other label that falls in the realm of "pathological," but it does cause us quite a lot of pain, confusion, and unhappiness.

Consider Diane, an accomplished writer in her mid-30s, who was having a hard time finding a guy with whom she could have a relationship. She had been married and divorced in her 20s. "The guy wasn't awful," she said, "but he was really hard to please, and I always felt like I was coming in second to his work."

Her parents were also smart and successful in their careers. Diane's mother, a physician, was the chief of surgery at a highly respected hospital. When Diane was about two years old, her mom went back to work full-time—"about eighty hours a week," Diane reported.

In retrospect, Diane's mother and father both agreed that those two years between Diane's birth and her mom's return to work were very tough on her mother. She had an unmistakable undercurrent of worry and impatience. On the surface this was attributed to the potential loss of the professional status for which she'd had to work very hard. Deeper down, as Diane and I talked more, it seemed to have been more about a basic need to have everything—including Diane—reflect well upon her.

Diane's dad was an artist with a studio in their house, and so Diane had a fair amount of time with him, but he, as Diane described him, "wasn't a touchy-feely kind of guy." If things didn't go well, she said, "he'd go sulk in front of the TV."

As we talked more about her relationships with her mom and dad, it was clear that Diane hadn't made a connection between those relationships and her present problems. She said, "I know they care about me and love me; they were affectionate and all that, and it's not like I was neglected or abused, so why are you saying that my parents are such a big deal in whether or not I can find somebody?"

Here's why. Imagine, from little Diane's viewpoint, that she felt her parents' love for her—but she also picked up on the other, more subtle but still powerful feelings in how her parents related to her. She sensed the undercurrent of Mom's anxiety and impatience and Dad's default mode of checking out.

Well, then, little Diane developed a brilliant strategy, deep wn in her brain, below conscious awareness: if she wanted to avoid the yucky feeling of her mom's anxiety and frustration whenever she spent time with her, she'd better be darn sure she was making her mom feel that having a kid had been worthwhile. Diane remembers being a pretty anxious kid, always trying to accumulate enough "A's and praise" in school to impress her mom (*See? I can make you feel good about yourself as a parent, so love me. Please?*).

And she made sure that she steered conversations with her Dad to nonemotional, intellectual areas in which he felt competent and good, so he wouldn't go off and disappear.

Now, from this perspective of Diane's early relationships with her parents, take a look again at her description of her ex-husband: "He was just really hard to please, and I always felt like I was coming in second to his work."

Her parents weren't evil, or abusive, or neglectful. Far from it—they were doing the best they could. They were probably simply doing what *their* parents had wired into *their* brains.

As babies and kids, we're all just trying to do the best we can with the hands we're dealt—the adaptation I talked about earlier—and our brains wire up accordingly. It turns out that these early attachment experiences not only have an effect on how unpleasant it might be to go home for Thanksgiving, but they also have longstanding effects on how your brain takes shape. Let me emphasize again that this doesn't make your parents the "bad guys," and this doesn't make you a victim; it just means you have some work to do to turn the ship around—which you can do!

In fact, you are now on your way to digging in and getting the job done right. The challenge—the responsibility, really—of adulthood is understanding that you can no longer use the same (albeit then-brilliant) strategies you developed in childhood, and then making the necessary repairs. For example, Diane kept trying to be the same kind of achiever-and-pleaser with her ex-husband as she'd been with her mom and dad—and her brain was probably unconsciously attracted to him in the first place because a hard-to-please person was her most familiar connection—but the old strategy wasn't working. Something needed to change.

Coming to that awareness, though, wasn't enough for Diane to break those "habits" her brain had wired up when she was a kid. Despite her intellectual understanding, and in spite of her best efforts to stop herself, the pattern kept repeating in all her relationships with men. Being really smart, putting ideas together, and other higher-level thinking strategies aren't enough on their own to bring about lasting change in how you live your life. (That's why reading self-help books is often so unhelpful in making lasting changes, even though they make so much sense.) You need to change the underlying wiring itself, and insight alone doesn't do that. It can shine a light on the issue—*aha!*—but it doesn't do the rewiring.

So that's the bad news.

But there is good news! You can do something about that old wiring. That's why you're reading this book!

Before we move into fixing things, though, it'll be helpful to know a little more about what you're dealing with: what was happening in that little baby brain of yours as the first big bundle of relationship wiring was being laid?

Crawling Inside: A Baby's Developing "Relationship Brain"

There your parents were, holding your tiny little newborn self. You weren't doing much, or so it seemed, other than eating and sleeping and crying and filling your diaper. In reality, though, you were one busy baby. From the time you were conceived, your brain was exploding with development, much of it in response to what you were experiencing. As babies, we're little attachment-experience sponges, with our brains taking in a huge amount of interpersonal data and transforming it into our earliest wiring for closeness. You could see this as a survival tool: being born exquisitely sensitive to whether we're safe or not, and using that to lay down the wiring accordingly.

Your brain is divided into two connected but differentiated ves, or hemispheres. We're hugely right-hemisphere-dominant when we're born, and the right hemisphere is the heavyweight champ when it comes to the earliest brain growth and activity.

For relationships, what does this mean? Well, let's look a little more at what we know about the right hemisphere's specialties (we'll get more into this later): It's where we "sense" feelings (ours and those of others). It's deeply connected to the viscera (our gut-organs) and the body, and it activates our emotions through our physiology. It understands things in a holistic, big-picture way, rather than breaking things down into smaller parts. It's very much into nonverbal information, such as body language and facial expressions. And it incorporates experiences as *implicit* memories. These are memories that are tapped into later when a current experience reminds us of something we've encountered before, and the tricky part is that they include old emotional information *without our being aware of it.* Another thing that makes implicit memories tricky is that they don't have any time-and-date stamp. They just "are," whenever your brain remembers them. When that happens, your left hemisphere, trying to be logical and helpful in making sense of your current experience, attributes the feelings evoked by the implicit memories to the present situation—and confabulates an explanation.

Let's say you went to the circus when you were a wee tot, and, like so many others, you were scared by the clowns—too much, too loud, too strange-looking for you. That feeling, which happened in the context of the circus, is stored in your implicit memory: *circus = yikes!*

Now let's say you're 25 and your first-time date has the bright idea of going to the circus. Probably without even realizing it, you start to feel a little anxious. Your adult, "rational" brain knows there's nothing scary at the circus (other than the price of the cotton candy), but still you just have this feeling that's been stirred, thanks to your implicit memory.

Because it's an implicit memory that is getting called up, you aren't aware that the feeling/memory you're having is about the circus from over 20 years ago—it feels like it's all about *now.* If *now* you're sitting with your date . . . well, pity the poor guy, because you're likely to attribute the "yikes" feeling to him. Consciously or not, it could go something like this: *Hmm, I'm feeling kind of icky and anxious right now, sitting here with this guy. Maybe I should dump him.*

So your old, deeply wired memories about safe/unsafe, move-close/run-for-the-hills are pulling the strings on you behind the scenes—and the vast majority of the time, you don't even know they're being pulled from the past. You feel it *now,* and so you attribute it to what's going on *now.*

Another important thing to keep in mind about implicit memories (which we'll get into in more detail in Chapter 7) is that they're driven by the deep, nonverbal, nonlogical parts of your brain that are intensely engaged with survival and fear. And whenever you try to untangle some of those behind-the-scenes strings, you do it the way we highly verbal humans try to solve every other kind of problem—by using the language-based, logical, *upper left* hemisphere in your conscious brain. Yet it's mostly your *lower right* hemisphere that's pulling the strings. That's like trying to negotiate a peace treaty with life forms on another planet when you have little or no contact with them and you don't speak the language. It's not gonna go well.

Baby's Got a Deep Brain

Another important aspect of baby brains to keep in mind as we talk about early relationships is that they're pretty basic. You know how we humans like to think we're superior to other mammals because we've got this fabulously wrinkly, highly evolved brain, and a really super-duper cortex (the part that presumably sets us "above" other primates)? Well, the thought-full cortex isn't running the show in young babies. They're not pondering the meaning of life or trying to understand trigonometry. Babies are mostly hanging out in the lower, deeper parts of their brains, which are focused more on survival.

Fear and its separated-at-birth twin, anger, are survival mechanisms, and so they're both wired in from the start. Of course, as a baby, if you're afraid, you can't run, and if you're angry, you can't say, "Yeah, well, same to you, moron!" and stomp off. You're stuck there with your parents, since your little life literally depends upon them for survival.

So how does the "baby you" deal with those basic, vital emotions? An example will show you (and reinforce just how influential your parents are in the way you will deal with relationships for the rest of your life).

Say you're a crying baby and your mom is holding you in her arms and singing to you. She's a bit tense. She just had a tiff with Dad, and she's exhausted because you kept her up most of last night. She's worried that if she can't soothe you, she'll go sleepless again tonight (and Dad will be even crankier tomorrow).

While she's singing and rocking and doing whatever else she can think of to calm you down, she's also thinking and feeling something like this, a pretty normal response to a crying baby, if we're honest about it: *Pleeeease stop crying. This is so frustrating! I'm exhausted! I love you, but you're a royal pain in the butt right now. I really want to be a good mother, but I can't seem to figure it out! I feel like an incompetent human being, and I hate that! Why can't I quiet a simple little baby? I went to college, for crying out loud!*

Also firing off are Mom's own implicit memory connections, the ones related to her own babyhood and maybe *her* mother's tension and impatience with *her* crying. And to make it even more challenging, her attachment style is coming on strong—which, let's say for this example, is based on the idea of needing to do things really, really well so that others will love her.

Mom's doing her best, holding you, singing, and probably not even consciously aware of most of the busyness in her brain, the tension in her arms, her increased heart rate, the fleeting emotions showing on her face. But you can bet your bottom dollar that you, the baby in her arms, so exquisitely sensitive to social and emotional cues, are taking it all in—feeling tone, body language, the whole deal.

In your right-brained, deep-brained baby wisdom, it goes something like this (although, obviously, not in words, and completely unconsciously):

I'm feeling and expressing the need for someone else to soothe me, and I'm getting a mixed response. There's this singing stuff, which is nice, and being held is good, but there's this tension and worry and, hmm, is that anger? They're all jumbled together. Yuck.

Ding! Here's our first implicit memory: *crying and being held is confusing and a little worrisome.*

(Of course, one bad night of crying with a stressed-out mother doesn't cause you, 30 years later, to shudder at the thought of turning to your partner when you're sad. Pathways are built by an accumulation of experiences.)

Since we've established that running away or telling your parents off can't happen until much later, what's a baby to do with all of this information? Baby brilliantly—but basically unconsciously—figures out the patterns of life with Mom and Dad and how to make the best of it.

That's where attachment styles come in.

How This Plays Out as You Grow Up: Attachment Styles

Recall from earlier that, for most people, there are two ways attachment can go: secure or insecure. If your parents "got it right" at least half the time, research shows you will probably have a healthy way with attachment. But chances are you're a member of the Insecure Attachment Club. I can be fairly confident about that, for two reasons: First, as mentioned before, nearly half of American adults fall into this category. Second, if you're having problems with relationships such that you're reading this book about how to make them better (or had someone hand it you, with a look that said, "You. Need. This."), it's an excellent bet that an insecure style of attachment has been in play.

It's a big camp, with lots of people like you—and me—with well-meaning parents who passed along some suboptimal ways of being in relationships.

It makes sense, then, that we'll be focusing first on insecure attachment, to more fully understand what we're up against. Since my firm stance as a psychologist is that I believe we're all capable of growth and healing, we'll also be spending plenty of time later on secure attachment and how to grow your own. And since I'm a neuroscience geek, we'll be looking at all of this through the lens of the brain.

Fear and Loathing in . . . Attachment

Your brain is constantly assessing your situation for safety/danger. If it determines that things are safe and good, then your body, via one part of your nervous system—the *parasympathetic nervous system*—is set to relaxation, receptivity, openness, flexibility, and connection to the world and people around you. You can slow down and take it all in.

But if the brain determines that things out there are unsafe or potentially painful, it activates a different part of your nervous system, the *sympathetic nervous system,* and the fight-or-flight reaction kicks in.

You can think of the sympathetic nervous system as the accelerator, the gas pedal—the thing that allows you to rev up to run or fight. The parasympathetic nervous system is the brake pedal; it slows you down. (You'll learn more about this later.)

With a good driving instructor (your parent), you can learn how to successfully slow down and speed up smoothly (healthy regulation of your emotions and impulses) and get the car to do what you need it to do.

How does your parent teach you this?

Take a look at a toddler who's just been surprised and a little hurt by a fall. Her sympathetic nervous system, the gas pedal, has accelerated a bit, but she's in that state where she's unsure if all-out alarm sounding is needed. Her dad is the kind of guy who's always working really hard to keep things controlled and quiet (maybe there was a lot of fear-inducing yelling when he was growing up). He's quickly at her side. "Oh, NO!" is the likely response of his own body's gas pedal, mashed down by both the sight of his baby girl having fallen and his need for her not to cry. As a result, when he tries to comfort her, he's already uptight; he's not able to engage any of the soothing brakes of *his* parasympathetic system. The little girl, in Dad's arms now (which would ordinarily give her body the signal to calm down and start using her own parasympathetic brakes) hears Daddy say in a fast, loud, tense voice, "You're okay! No need to cry! It doesn't hurt!" She doesn't respond by immediately cheering up. Dad quickly starts to feel even more inadequate and uptight. His sympathetic nervous system is so keyed up at this point that he gets irritated and scolds her ("fight") and then, in his fear and shame about having scolded her and being a bad father after all, he leaves the room ("flight"). That's going to feel unsafe and confusing to this little girl, leaving her with a gas pedal and brakes that are confusing to regulate.

If this is a familiar, repeated pattern, this kid's brain will create wiring pathways that cause her to have some degree of anxiety/fear in response to closeness.

Hold Me Close, Pleeeeease?

In the example above, the toddler could work really hard to stay in connection with her dad, unconsciously (and nonverbally) going for something like this: *I'm really a very good girl, and I'll please you and make you feel better about yourself, just please love me and don't leave me.*

That'd be anxious attachment: working hard to convince someone to love you and stay with you. And remember that for these earliest experiences, there's no time-and-date stamp. The unconscious lesson, incorporated well and deeply, is this: *If I want people to love me and stay close to me, I need to please them and do whatever it takes to get them to stick around.*

Remind you of anyone you know? About 20 percent of American adults show this anxious style of insecure attachment, although most don't know it. Those of us with an anxious attachment style tend to seek intimate closeness—sometimes to a very high degree; we seem to crave approval and responsiveness from our significant others, and can often become pretty emotionally dependent. At the same time that we want/need a lot of closeness, we actually tend to be pretty distrustful of the whole deal (*is it safe?*), which leads to a lot of worry, busyness, and impulsiveness (*I know I said I wasn't going to call, but I just couldn't help myself*). Expression of emotion tends to run pretty high, while self-esteem is often quite low. All of this, remember, fits with the anxiety about wanting to be close, but feeling that "close" is a risky place, rife with the possibility of rejection and abandonment. Wanting love so badly that you end up losing it is a confusing way to live. (Albert Brooks's character in *Broadcast News* said it best: "Wouldn't it be great if we lived in a world where insecurity and desperation made us more attractive?")

Steer Clear

Our unhappy little toddler could also take another tack: *Uh-oh, here comes Dad and that closeness stuff again. That never goes well. I need him, but when he tries to make me feel better, he always ends up mad at me and walks away. That hurts. Who wants that again? I'll just be quiet and keep my needs to myself.*

That'd be avoidant attachment. The deeply ingrained, unconscious lesson here is: *I'm not going to reach out and show that I need anyone. Getting close to people is unlikely to make me feel better, and will probably make me feel worse. I'll be just fine as long as I keep a big emotional distance from others.*

This probably sounds familiar to you as well. The research shows that 25 percent of American adults have this avoidant style of insecure attachment—again, usually without their awareness. Sometimes holding independence up like a trophy, those of us with this style often prefer to see ourselves as self-sufficient and not needful of close relationships. Emotions are very often shunted to the background, and even if we put ourselves out there enough to experience the pain of rejection, we can do things like "rationalize the feeling away" by thinking poorly of an emotionally "needy" former partner. Another form of this self-protectiveness sometimes results in having the desire for closeness, but feeling so uncomfortable and mistrustful of it—and seeing ourselves as so undeserving of it—that we avoid it and try to bury our hunger for it.

Because these early experiences are pretty ordinary, we tend to be unaware that they're in any way significant in shaping our brains and our attachment styles. Most of us simply say, "Well, that's just who I am," as if it's a done deal and can't ever change. But your brain can change, and by changing it, you can have more joy and ease in connections and relationship.

Anxious, Meet Avoidant.
Avoidant, This Is Anxious.

What may sound really familiar to you is when these two types of attachment styles meet up and decide to have a relationship.

Unbeknownst to her, Ann has an anxious style of attachment. Her mother was consistently anxious about how Ann was doing as a child, and as a result her mother was emotionally needy and intrusive.

Not surprisingly, Ann tends to pay a lot of attention—consciously and unconsciously—to what other people around her are feeling or needing, and she enjoys being thoughtful, generous, and considerate. She likes to feel appreciated and can be a little hypersensitive if someone is displeased with her.

One fine day she meets Steve, who grew up with an avoidant attachment style. His parents basically steered clear of Steve's (and their own) inner, emotional life and tended to dismiss all of that "talking-about-feelings nonsense." Above all, they prized intellectual discourse and a cool head.

At first, being with Steve felt great to Ann: he wasn't intrusive at all; he was independent, had his own interests, and was certainly not clinging or needy as her mother had been.

For Steve, Ann's emotional openness and generosity were wonderful, welcome antidotes to his own rather cold, aloof parents. She seemed to "get" his feelings, which he appreciated, because he'd long felt unseen and misunderstood.

Sounds like a good match, right?

Flash forward about two years. We find Ann and Steve in my office for couples' therapy (Steve, very reluctantly so). Ann is fed up with Steve's emotional distance and refusal to commit to a deeper relationship. Steve says that Ann's emotionality and constant demands for affection and approval are driving him nuts.

There You Have It

So now you can really understand how deeply (literally and figuratively) your earliest experiences of relationships have shaped you in being able to find and have a relationship with Mr. or Ms. Right. I hope you also understand a bit more about why recent findings that you can change the shape and wiring of your brain are so exciting. We've all been given a second chance.

And now that you've read this chapter, you know that all of us who have struggled to engage in self-improvement or to increase our self-acceptance—or any other method for trying to make healthier relationships with ourselves and others possible—have been going about the problem a bit backward. We've been trying to get our cortex, the intellectual part perched way atop our brains, to make changes in the way the deep, lower parts of our brains drive our relationships.

If we can bring a bit more integration between these parts of our brains, we can bridge that communication gap. And your brain has the perfect structures for that very task—they're probably just not buff, brawny, and connected enough. In order to make the best use of the latest neuroscience to bulk them up, we're going to need just a bit more familiarity with those helpful but as yet underdeveloped parts.

Let's move on to Chapter 2 and take a look at the inside of your brain, so you can see which parts and pathways we're wanting—and able—to build up and rewire using mindfulness meditation.

CHAPTER 2

WHAT GOES WHERE

The Wiring Diagram of the Relationship Brain

Time to get down with your geek self. First, take a nice, easy breath. You may have had previous negative experiences and frightening biology teachers who showed you hideously difficult diagrams of the brain, and the sheer overwhelming feeling of "WTF?!!" might understandably have shut down your ability to think altogether.

So we'll make this simple enough to understand, simple enough to keep your fear buttons from getting pushed, and simple enough to let you build on top of these pieces of your brain in ways that support healthier, more vibrant relationships.

That's my guiding principle in teaching this to my patients: I provide insight into the brain in service of creating a greater capacity for healthy, vibrant relationships.

As neuroanatomist Marian Diamond, PhD, said: "May knowledge of the brain provide people of all nations with greater tolerance, empathy, and appreciation of human behavior."[1]

Diamond might not approve, however, of the first thing I'm going to do: ignore a lot of major chunks of the brain and many of its multitudinous functions. I'm going to focus here on just five "parts" of the brain and two important brain-integration pathways specific to our purpose: helping you to understand your relationship brain and wiring it for optimal functioning.

Five "parts" and two pathways. Nothing needs to be memorized. You can do this.

Basics about How the Brain Works

Before we dive into the "parts," you'll want to know something about some underlying principles of the brain. What we'll cover here isn't comprehensive neurology, just what will be helpful for you to know when it comes to your relationship brain. There are three basic principles I'd like to discuss before we focus on the "parts."

Principle Number One: The brain isn't made up of discrete "parts" with a single job. You'll notice that so far I've been putting the word *parts* in quotes (after this paragraph, I promise I'll stop). That's because as much as we'd like it to be so when we're trying to understand the brain, the way the brain works isn't like your computer—keyboard does X, processor does Y, software does Z. In your lusciously complex brain, *parts* and *functions* and even *systems* and *circuits* almost all belong in quotation marks, because all those terms are a bit misleading. Sometimes, what look like separate brain parts actually function as a unit; other times, what looks like one distinct part might actually be doing a number of different things and have distinctly different subunits belonging to different systems. It's not as straightforward as "this part does this, that part does that." For the purposes of this book, I'll refer to structures and systems by how they participate in our relationships, but keep in mind that cooperation, communication, and healthy interdependence are vitally important in how your brain functions (and they're vital concepts in how relationships work as well. Nice how that works).

Principle Number Two: Your nervous system is organized (Congratulations!). At its most basic level, you can look at it as a series of branches, kind of like a tree: You've got the sort of "central" part of your nervous system—your brain and your spinal cord—which tends to get most of the attention, much like the trunk of a tree. But your nervous system also has another very important part: your *peripheral nervous system.*

Now divide this peripheral nervous system into two branches: your *autonomic system* and your *somatic system.*

Your autonomic system is the important one for our purposes here. Focus in on it and you'll see that it, too, has two major branches: your *sympathetic system* (which, despite its name, isn't about sympathy), and your *parasympathetic* system.

- Your **sympathetic** system's duties have to do with responding to threats and other things that motivate you—it gets you moving, revved up, like the accelerator of an engine. Remember the example of the falling toddler and her father from Chapter 1. She fell, and her father's sympathetic system fueled him to run to her side to make sure she wasn't hurt.
- Your **parasympathetic** system is all about getting your body to slow back down, like the brakes on your car—to get your body to conserve energy, make necessary repairs, and recover from the stress that your sympathetic responses have caused.

Those two branches are all that's typically talked about in neurology, but—and I really like this—you also have what's called the *smart vagus* (also called the *social engagement system*), which can be thought of as a third branch of your autonomic nervous system; it sort of parallels your parasympathetic system. We'll be talking more about your smart vagus, but for now, know that it's a really good buddy when it comes to relationships—it is dedicated to helping you fine-tune your body's reactions, especially when it comes to making connections in the social world. That soft look in your eyes, the mellowing of your voice . . . ahhh. Thanks, smart vagus.

Principle Number Three: Your brain and nervous system communicate through electricity and chemicals passed between cells. *Neurons* are cells of varying sizes, shapes, and sensitivities. These nifty little units receive and send signals—bits of information—using electrical impulses and chemical messengers (*neurotransmitters*). The tiny bits of information are communicated from one neuron to others in a staggeringly complex network; there are about 100 billion neurons in your brain, and each one has between 10 and 20,000 connections (*synapses*) with other neurons. (It always fascinates me that every second of every day, my brain manages this network of trillions of connections, and yet I can't even wrap my brain around what exactly a "trillion" is.)

Another aspect of your nervous system's method of communication is that it works with "on" signals as well as "off" signals, known respectively as *excitation* and *inhibition.* These signals happen at the "micro" level of neurons—a particular neuron might be "excited" by one neurotransmitter and "inhibited" by another. Excitation and inhibition happen at a more "macro" level, too. For example, the front part of your brain (having to do with conscious thought) has bundles of neurons that reach down to your lower brain (having to do with emotional reactivity) and deliver a neurochemical off-switch, which means that you can use your awareness to inhibit or regulate your emotional responses.

There's another aspect to communication within your brain that's a really huge deal, which I mentioned earlier: *neuroplasticity.* Thanks to both Donald Hebb, PhD (a psychologist considered to be one of the fathers of neuropsychology), and Nobel Prize–winning neuropsychiatrist Eric Kandel, MD, we know that experience physically changes the connections in your brain. Pathways get set up. Wiring gets laid down. Your brain has the capacity, *throughout your lifespan,* to change its very structure and organization, to change the pathways of communication—simply through the active communication between your neurons.

Neurons communicate, getting one another fired up, and *neurons that fire together, wire together* (a principle known as "Hebb's rule"), changing the structure and function of your brain. Change can happen in a number of different ways: making new connections between neurons (structural change); creating new neural pathways (functional change); and growing new neurons, called *neurogenesis.* We're still discovering how, when, and where neurogenesis happens—but what seems certain is that *experience* is one of the primary ways that you can stimulate neurogenesis in your own brain. *What you do and what you think sculpt your brain.* Two neighboring neurons firing together repeatedly (let's say, as you're learning your way around a new city) become more efficient at firing together.

It's also important to keep in mind that neurons, connections, and pathways that don't get used can be pruned, or die off (since, like people, a neuron needs to be stimulated and connected in order to survive and thrive). "Use it or lose it" is one way to think about this aspect of neuroplasticity. Whichever pathways get the most traffic, that's where your brain spends its highway budget to build faster, wider, and more complex highways—while the other roads get rutted and abandoned.

Parts of the Brain

Now that you understand those three important principles, I'm going to take you briefly through each of the brain parts that have a role in relationships. As these parts become important in subsequent chapters, I'll walk you through more information about them that'll be useful in understanding how your brain does relationships. Please follow along on the diagram on page 25.

As you're reviewing each of the parts, remember that neuroscientists know more about some of these structures than they do about others; sometimes, the deeper a structure is in the human brain, the longer the investigation of it can take, and the more complicated it may seem to be. Paying attention to the sometimes "fuzzy," still-debated deeper parts of the brain is definitely worth the effort for you, though, in your growth toward better relationships. This is because for anything to really change how you live your life (including how you do your relationships), it has to change your brain at multiple levels, not just in the "thinking" areas that get busy when you learn a new fact or put ideas together. The deeper in the brain the changes are, the more transformative they seem to be. The deeper structures, as you'll see, have much to do with emotional reactions and your ability to regulate them in ways that work better for you in relationships.

Again, that's why being incredibly smart, learning a lot from self-help books, or making resolutions often doesn't bring about changes in your life or your relationships that "stick." They don't change your brain in the deep structures. Mindfulness meditation? There's more and more evidence that it can, and does.

Okay, take another easy breath, let it out, and take a look at your relationship-brain parts list.

Amygdala: Your amygdala is a key player in your emotional life. (You actually have a pair of them, one on each side of your brain, but we'll keep it singular and simple.) The main job of the amygdala is to make an immediate assessment of safety or danger and to tell you whether you should feel scared or angry. Your amygdala responds in about 50 milliseconds—about *half* of an eye blink. (Your more complex and "thinking" cortex takes about ten times as long—500 to 550 milliseconds—to come up with conscious awareness of what your amygdala has already reacted to.) If a lion is chasing you, without needing to kick it up to your highfalutin cortex (which would waste valuable time), the danger-switch in your amygdala is flipped on, and *zing!* Your amygdala sends the alarm to the rest of the brain to start spitting out messages (chemical and electrical) that will get you to run before you even have a chance to think.

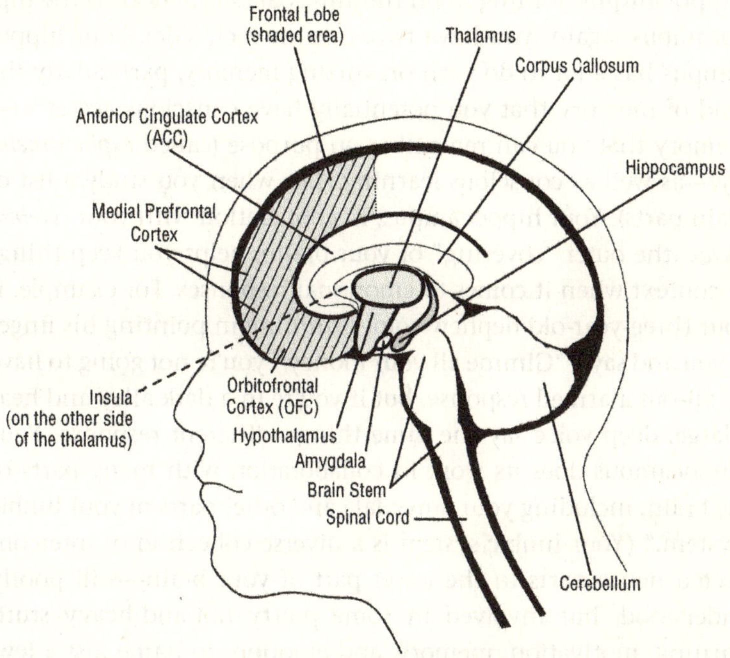

(Note on diagram: What you're looking at here is a flat map of a three-dimensional, multilayered object. If you were to slice your brain in half like an avocado (don't try this at home), you wouldn't see these structures all lined up along the cut surface—some would be hidden behind the "pit," for example. What this diagram does do, though, is show you the relative geographical relationships between these structures of the "relationship brain.")

The amygdala also plays a role in the formation of your earliest, "preconscious" memories (the memories from before age two or three), as well as (we think) memories of traumatic events in adulthood—the *implicit memory* mentioned earlier. Your amygdala also seems to be necessary for developing and expressing trust. The list goes on: It has a critical part in decision-making, and it's deeply involved in your responses to emotional stimuli. And last but definitely not least, your amygdala is a big player in the neural networks that handle *attachment*—how you relate to those people with whom you have relationships.

Hippocampus: Joining in on the amygdala's functions is the hippocampus (again, you have two, one on each side). Your hippocampus has a lot to do with organizing memory, particularly the kind of memory that you potentially have conscious access to—memory that you can remember on purpose (called *explicit memory)*—as well as conscious learning (like when you study a list of brain parts). Your hippocampus, in cooperation with your *cerebral cortex* (the outer "covering" of your brain), helps you keep things in context when it comes to emotional responses. For example, if your three-year-old nephew comes running in pointing his finger at you and says, "Gimme all your money," you're not going to have an all-out alarmed response, but if you're in a dark alley and hear a large, deep voice say the same thing—different response. Your hippocampus does its work in collaboration with many parts of the brain, including your amygdala and other parts of your limbic "system." (Your limbic system is a diverse collection of interconnected neuro-parts in the lower part of your brain—still poorly understood, but involved in some pretty hot-and-heavy stuff: learning, motivation, memory, and emotion, to name just a few. For our purposes, we'll mostly focus on just two limbic structures: your amygdala and your hippocampus.)

Insula: Tucked in between what look like the outer layers of the brain and the deepest inner structures, so that you'd have to lift the "roof" of your brain (your frontal lobe) and pull back the side "wing" (one of your temporal lobes, on the sides) to get a peek at it, is the insula.

The insula itself isn't all that's shrouded; its functions and mechanisms of influence are still a bit of a mystery as well. Neuroanatomists aren't sure whether to call it its own lobe, part of the temporal lobe, or part of the limbic system (which, as I mentioned earlier, is a big hairy mess anyway). That dispute, if nothing else, gives you an idea of how much of a hand the insula has in various pots.

We know that your insula keeps the lines of communication open between your inner and outer experiences of your body and your emotions, linking your higher-level "thinking" cortex and your more purely "emotional" limbic region. It gets active when you experience pain—in yourself or in someone else—and seems to be involved in what your emotional response to the pain will be. Given that, you can see why we think it's involved in attachment.

Sometimes called the "limbic integration cortex," it also seems to help you know the difference between what you're experiencing and what someone else is experiencing. That might seem like a "duh" kind of thing—but that's because your insula is on the job. (Imagine seeing someone you care about dropping a heavy object on his toe—you feel a version of "ouch" too, as I mentioned above. Now imagine that you can't tell the difference between his pain and yours—your response to his pain would be pretty screwy. Without your insula, you wouldn't know the difference.)

This supports the findings that the insula seems to be a key player in your capacity for empathy—a rather important ingredient in healthy relationships, as we'll see later on.

The front (anterior) part of your insula also seems to play an important role in social connections, having to do with cooperation[2]—sustaining it and repairing it.

Now, here's a very handy thing to know about the insula: The right anterior insula has been found in at least one study to be significantly thicker in people who meditate.[3] Tuning in to your own sensations, or attuning to those of another, gets your insula nice and dense—and more active.

Anterior cingulate cortex: Your anterior cingulate cortex (ACC), together with your insula, acts like a sort of balancing middleman. With the insula, your anterior cingulate is a player in the interface between the *cortical* parts (the upper, sort of "thinking" part of your brain) and the *subcortical* parts (your lower, more "raw-feeling" brain parts, like your amygdala). It judges what's most important right now in your body, in your immediate environment, or the people you're with. You might be standing in a sandwich shop (which, at lunchtime, is a busy, chaotic environment), hungry for lunch (your internal state being hunger)—and if the child in your arms (your interpersonal connection) suddenly starts to cry, your cingulate will help you allocate your attention to where it's most needed at the moment. Even just one part of the cingulate, the anterior (front) portion, seems to have its spoon stirring in many pots, including emotional regulation, the ability to recognize one's emotions, and motivation to communicate with others. All relationship biggies, yes?

The anterior cingulate is one of very few areas in the brain that has been shown to have von Economo neurons (or VENs), which seem to play a major role in our capacity for empathy,[4] one of the biggest of the relationship biggies.

Orbitomedial prefrontal cortex: As far as the relationship brain is concerned, one very important area is the orbitomedial prefrontal cortex (OMPFC). Why is it important? Simply put, it's well placed, and it's got some incredibly important connections.

First of all, your OMPFC is part of your frontal cortex. Your frontal cortex is pretty big (you're welcome), located at the front and top of your brain, behind your forehead.

Now, zoom in on your frontal cortex and you'll see the part that's way up front: the *prefrontal cortex*. Your PFC is heavily involved in what we think of as "thinking": higher-level reasoning, planning, organization, directing your attention, holding back your impulses, and other actions that lead us to call the PFC the "CEO" of the brain. It does its job using information fed to it by other parts of the brain, including emotional, sensory, and motor information, as well as memories. It's important in being able to think abstractly, to have flexibility in your thinking when new information comes in, and to be able to imagine the feelings of others—to consider someone else's perspective, to try to figure out "where they're coming from." Those are pretty key ingredients in relationships.

And finally, snuggled at the bottom of the prefrontal cortex, directly above your eyes and set back a bit, is your OMPFC. It's almost like it's stuck onto the bottom "ledge" of your frontal cortex. This, as it turns out, is a very cool position to do a lot of things.

These will be discussed as we move through the chapters that follow, but for now, take a look at a few OMPFC factoids:

- According to some, the OMPFC holds dual citizenship in your limbic system and your cortex, allowing it to bridge the gap between the two. That's a little like managing to be a cool kid *and* a nerd.
- The OMPFC sits on top of (and connects in major ways with) deeper brain structures involved in emotions, such as your amygdala and your anterior cingulate.
- Tactless? Inappropriate? Restless? Quick-tempered? Maybe depressed, unmotivated, and listless? These are symptoms that might be seen if your OMPFC gets knocked offline.
- Your OMPFC plays an important role in relationships because it is a key structure in gathering and processing "social information." It helps your brain as a whole make decisions on how to respond (Do I yell now? Do I move away? Do I think for a moment more?). If you see a facial expression that looks like someone who is about to blow her top, you can thank your OMPFC for helping you draw on context and previous experiences—allowing you to calculate your reaction based on whether the face belongs to your scary exploding boss or your two-month-old niece.

Now I'm going to offer you a little bit of a "cheat." We're going to be talking a fair amount about the three parts we just covered—the insula, the ACC, and the OMPFC—and so it can be helpful from time to time to use a sort of shorthand term that combines them all. Daniel Siegel, MD suggests the "middle prefrontal cortex." Others, like Lennart Heimer, MD, call this the *basal forebrain.*[5] It's not an actual anatomical part, nothing that you could dissect from the brain or look up in a neuroanatomy atlas and say, "Aha! Here it is!" But given the complexity of all of this, my patients have appreciated a simple collective name for these parts, so we'll use "basal forebrain," bringing together aspects of the orbital-medial-frontal areas, the anterior cingulate, and the insula—as a shorthand for these important integration-team members.

Putting the Parts Together

Much of our emotional well-being hinges, it seems, on having a brain that isn't constantly at odds with itself or the world. An *integrated* brain is the way to go. I want to highlight some of this integration here, and we'll definitely be talking more about it later on.

This "putting the parts together" section will start to help you understand more about the amazing and intricate "sum is greater than the whole" beauty of your brain. Brain parts aren't just distinct, lone-acting pieces soldered together; information in your brain doesn't just bop along in a *foot-bone's-connected-to-the-ankle-bone* manner. Obviously, it's vastly more complicated than that. You've got to start somewhere, though, so I'll tell you about just a couple of basic dimensions of integration.

Second, because there are so many perspectives from which to look at the intricate, complex, and as-yet-minimally-understood pathways in the brain, I'm going to keep the discussion here limited to "from the emotional and relationship well-being standpoint." So, when I talk about the right hemisphere, for example, it'll be from the perspective of the right hemisphere's role in emotions and relationships—not the whole gloriously messy shebang.

So let's take a look at how the parts you learned about fit together into different pathways. We'll keep it simple and limit ourselves to just two.

Pathway Number One—Right-Left/Left-Right: Your right hemisphere's big jobs (when it comes to relationships) might be summed up this way: *body sensation, raw emotions (like anger and fear), and danger assessment.* Information coming in from your body is more the purview of the right hemisphere of your brain. Your right hemisphere is also more involved with your basic, emotional, unprocessed brain functions. The more primitive emotions that help us to survive—anger and fear, for example—arise more obviously from the right hemisphere. The right hemisphere dominates the left when it comes to defending you, leaving you likely to have your stress, fear, and anxiety (as well as pain) generally trump whatever "good" stuff might be going on in the left hemisphere. *Fight-flight-freeze* is heavily loaded on the right side of your brain.

If you're too heavily dependent on the right prefrontal area, according to Richard Davidson, PhD, you're also more likely to be overly cautious, risk-avoidant, and generally more anxious and fearful. Getting motivated to make your life happen can be a big challenge when your right prefrontal cortex runs the show.

All is not lost! Compare and contrast all of that raw, fear-based, survivalist right-hemisphere activity with your left hemisphere (think *logical, linear, language-based*). Your left hemisphere has a tremendous capacity to help you approach social connectedness (rather than withdraw, as your right hemisphere would tell you to do). It also affords you "positive" feelings like the motivation to go after meaningful goals, the appreciation of beauty, the sense of connection and affiliation, "getting" humor, the joy of winning a game, and much, much more. Your left hemisphere also has the "advantage" of being more densely hooked up with your higher-level, cortical thinking and reasoning, and it quite literally has language on its side—so you might think of the left as having the potential to be the "pen" that is mightier than the right hemisphere's "sword."

Even some of the downsides to being more left-hemisphere-inclined are pretty good. While you might be more susceptible to getting cranky if your higher motivation hits an obstacle, that works in the left hemisphere to get you moving and energized to move past the block. Davidson goes so far as to say that left prefrontal activity is what gives us our sense of purpose in life and the motivation to go pursue it.

Getting your right and left hemispheres to work together is imperative in increasing your capacity for healthy relationships. As just one small example, if you're going to be aware of the feelings that your right hemisphere is handling (like fear or anger) and put them into conscious thoughts and words (activities that the left hemisphere oversees), you're going to need to pull the abilities of both hemispheres together. By applying Hebb's rule—firing together and wiring together—you'll be wiring new neural pathways between your right and left hemispheres.

So: *By practicing the recognition of your right-hemisphere feelings in the moment, and putting them into left-hemisphere words, you, my friend, are integrating your brain.*

That same principle applies to balancing your positive and negative emotions as well. Since we are rather fond of surviving, most of us walk around with a right-hemisphere bias—negative moods, fear, and so on. Studies on mindfulness meditators have shown, though, that their brain activity is shifted toward greater left-hemisphere activation. Better balance! Fear and gloom do not need to rule!

Big, big stuff.

Now let's look at *vertical integration*—also known as "top-down/bottom-up."

Pathway Number Two—Top-Down/Bottom-Up: The "top" of your brain—your *cerebral cortex*—is basically all that wrinkly stuff that you've seen in pictures and plastic models. In a relationship and emotional well-being context, the part of your cortex that we're most interested in is that highly integrative area called the OMPFC—which you already know something about. The OMPFC has a lot of connections, and as far as emotions go, one of its most important connections is with the amygdala—a bottom-dweller in your brain.

Your amygdala just might be the biggest "driver" of problems you encounter in relationships. Located deep down near the "bottom" of your brain, it tends to hang out with the dark, negative, painful emotions. Put that together with it being so vigilant, swift, and powerful in its declarations of threat, and it can really rule—and ruin—the day. For some of us, getting our amygdala to "shut up already!" is a Sisyphean task—pushing the boulder almost to the top of the mountain only to have it steamroll you on the way back down.

Fortunately, there are dense connections running back and forth between your "top of the brain" OMPFC and your lower-down amygdala. This lets your conscious, "reasoning" brain have access to what's going on in the trenches, while giving it the ability to modulate and temper your emotional responses. Affective neuroscience research, like studies from Davidson's group, suggests that we each have our own "balance" (or lack thereof) between the top and bottom, and this is, in large part, what shapes what we might call our emotional style and our M.O. for navigating relationships. If you tend to be "bottom-heavy," your emotional life will likely be more depressed and anxious. Integrate it with your "upper" brain and you increase your potential for a wider range of emotions and reactions, including empathy, humor, joy, and connection. It's a bit like changing your set point for your emotional life.

As a really basic way of summing this up: *right-left integration* allows you to get your raw emotions put more clearly into thoughts and words, without being ruled by Spock-like unemotionality, and *top-down integration* affords you more insight into (and control over) your unprocessed, unconscious reactivity, without diminishing your spunk and spontaneity.

Before we leave these first two pathways (*right-left/left-right* and *top-down/bottom-up*), take a moment to note that they aren't operating like two nonintersecting model train sets. The *top and left* areas, as I've described them here, tend to be more heavily wired with one another (think of the combo as intellectual and articulate and "reasonable," dealing with things like conscious awareness, being rational, and using your words). Similarly, the *bottom and right* areas (primal and wordless and emotionally intense, hanging together for what we think of as unconscious, body-based, emotional, nonverbal functions) also tend to be more heavily hooked up.

Just to keep things lively, both of these pathways also team up with many other structures, and each of *those* has important roles and influences. We'll come back to this later, so for now, just appreciate the complexity. (Or, if you feel the need to, curse it; I realize that your brain's intricacy may not seem like your friend just yet.)

By now, I'm sure you've gotten the point that you need to have it "goin' on" in multiple directions to have a vibrant, vital life. In the interest of keeping it simple, now that you've gotten a sense of the "why" and "where," you can focus on the idea of bringing together your upper-left brain with your lower-right brain. To paraphrase Shakespeare: *The integration's the thing!*

Let's move on, then, and get you wiring yourself up.

PART II

Becoming Your Own Master ELECTRICIAN

Essential Relationship Wiring Features
and How to Power Them Up

CHAPTER 3

Rewiring the Alarm Button

Body Regulation

Body regulation? What on earth do your heart rate, or the muscles in your middle ear (yes, really), have to do with healthier love and better relationships? And why start here?

Fair questions. And here are two questions for you: Have you ever tried to have a conversation with your partner and feel connected when you're feeling uptight because you're walking through a bad neighborhood? Or felt your heart race and your stomach tighten up—and lose your ability to think straight—when you've had a fight with your significant other?

The state of your body is connected to your state of mind, through your brain. It's also true in the other direction: your state of mind is connected to your body state. The less aware you are of what's going on in your body, and the more it just "does its thing" unchecked, the more likely that your basic, primitive, reflexive body states are going to be running the show in your relationships.

Not even the most amazing Baryshnikov moves by the rest of your brain stand a chance if your body state is swinging like a wild wrecking ball.

That's why we're starting here, in the body.

Let's take two examples of bodily reactions related to unpleasant external events: getting hit with a snarky comment from your significant other and hearing the sound of a gunshot. In both of these, your body perceives the sound, your brain responds (interpreting the words and tone of voice, or the source and proximity of the shot—then quickly sending messages out about how to physically react), and last (yes, last) but not least, you experience thoughts and feelings about the external events. You have an automatic physical and emotional "knee-jerk reaction" to potential danger, even before you're consciously aware of what's happened.

In relationships, what constitutes "danger" can be due to wiring that goes back millennia. For example, the "danger" of being emotionally abandoned comes from a time when mammals such as humans needed to be in close, safe units in order to survive and reproduce. (A cavewoman whose wiring led her to be happy and delighted at being thrown out on her own was unlikely to live very long, or to make cave-babies who were like her.)

So when a relationship "danger" comes up, whether subtle or huge, it's as if our bodies (including our brains) have been on the receiving end of that obnoxious little reflex hammer at the doctor's office. Hit*KICK*. Hit*KICK*.

A knee-jerk reaction in the literal sense—when the doctor dings your knee with that hammer and your leg goes flying up on its own—happens without your thinking about it. Your conscious brain doesn't even know what happened until after your leg has already responded.

The same is true for your body's reactions to emotional hammer-dings.

Hmmm. So what if you could regulate your knee-jerk bodily reactions to those emotional dings and avoid getting tangled up in automatic reactivity? You'd be better able to perceive most of the day-to-day "dangers" of being in a relationship as challenges for growth instead of threats. You might also be less defensive, better able to hear and respond to what's actually going on in the moment. That could lead to being more receptive to genuine connection and better able to foster it. Oh, and you'd be able to be more emotionally present, which would make for a better emotional connection, as well as a better sexual connection, with your partner.

Bottom line: if you can regulate and be tuned in to your body's reactions, you stand a far better chance to make mindful, healthier, more loving connections.

Keeping the Alarm Button "On": Michelle

Michelle scrambled to get her briefcase together at the end of a "day from hell" at the office. Truth be told, Michelle felt like every day at the office was a day from hell. She strapped on stress like a solo backpacker prepping for a year-long stint on the Appalachian Trail. And her life often felt like an endless, lonely mountain climb—even when she was in a relationship, like the one she'd been in for almost a year now, with Rob. She found it exasperating, exhausting, and ultimately depressing trying to be with someone, with a track record of long stretches of singlehood punctuated by a few painful relationships. She wanted to be in a healthy relationship so badly, but they were always so hard. (That was why she'd started working with me in psychotherapy three months earlier.)

On this particular day, Michelle's emotional backpack held some extra stress—she was headed to meet Rob after work, in an effort to have a date, which Rob thought might spark their dwindling romance. She couldn't tell what she was dreading more: succeeding in saving the relationship—which would mean more intimacy, leading to feeling even more scared of losing Rob—or ruining it now and being dumped and alone right away. Yeah, fun choices.

She hurried to catch—but ended up missing—the next subway train, and her heart was racing. It was hard to tell how much of that was from her sprint down the escalator and how much was from her anxious anticipation of the date. She felt as if the only thing she really craved at the moment was to be at home, alone, in some peace and quiet—and then she angrily criticized herself for wanting to be such a hermit. *Grow up already, Michelle. Time to stop hiding in your room. Rob is a good guy, and—the biggest point in his favor—he hasn't dumped you. Woo-hoo!—sort of.* The moment Rob had suggested having a "real date"—dinner out, conversation, the whole thing—Michelle had felt the small but undeniable clench in her stomach, along with the tension of saying yes, surpassed only by the loneliness of saying no.

So there she was, bracing herself for the date. She hated dates because they always seemed to backfire. She ended up trying too hard, wanting so much for things to go well that she'd get awkward and stuck, which made her feel like an idiot, and then she'd get irritable . . . a vicious cycle. *Just call him and reschedule,* she thought. *No, that'll just prolong the inevitable.* She held on more tightly to the pole in the subway car, her grip a bit slippery because of her sweaty palm.

She tried to reason with herself: *There's nothing to be worried about. You're looking forward to this, and everything's perfectly okay. Nothing to be worried about.* Somehow the reassurance made it worse, not better, twisting her anxiety even more.

When she arrived (15 minutes late, despite her best effort), the restaurant was crowded, the hostess was obnoxious, and as Michelle approached the table where Rob was seated, she was sure she saw it—*oh, yeah, it was there, even if just for a second*—an annoyed look on Rob's face. Even as she made herself walk toward the table, Michelle felt herself freeze inside, feeling ashamed and scared/frustrated/angry that she was about to blow this relationship too. She felt the beginning of a headache, like she'd gotten on almost all their other dates. *Oh, and now he's pretending that he's glad to see me. Great.*

Even if you didn't know anything about the brain, you'd probably be able to guess how Michelle and Rob's date went from there, and whether it helped the relationship, as Rob had hoped.

(Answers: *Badly* and *No.*) While they did patch things together enough to have sex later that night, Michelle was, as usual, lost in her anxiety about what had happened, what it meant for their future. They both ended up mostly just going through the motions. Again.

By knowing more about the brain and its various accessories, though, you'll understand more about why dates (and relationships) tended to go so badly for Michelle and what was going on in her wiring that made her body resemble an alarm system run amok. And—like Michelle, after she and I had worked together—you'll have some better ideas about what you can do to rewire the way your body responds to the stress of relationships and change the way it impacts your love life.

"Incoming!!"

Day in and day out, we scan our surroundings for information and our attention is grabbed by danger—we're innately wired that way. It's simply more basic to our survival than scanning and perceiving pleasant things—so it's no wonder, at the end of the day, that we can typically recall more tales of trouble than of pleasure. Fear trumps joy, and danger trumps pleasure, because fear and danger have more to do with our survival. Your job now, though, is to shift from living in *survive* mode too much of the time, and more into *thrive* mode. This is no small challenge: the tide of perceived danger—and of stress—is chronically high in our daily lives (think of driving in traffic, as just one example), so sometimes all it takes is a little extra stress—a bad interaction with your spouse after a long day at work—and you've reached flood levels, without so much as a sandbag to protect your relationship.

As the product of our biological evolution, and our bodies' "prime directive" to keep us safe and alive, we're wired to automatically detect and physically react to anything we perceive as a threat to our well-being—there's that knee-jerk reaction. And this is where the amygdala comes in. Without any thinking, *Danger!* is the assessment made by the amygdala, rapidly followed by a cascade of neurochemicals and hormones carrying messages that allow us to react immediately to that danger.

No doubt you've experienced some of these fight-or-flight reflexes: your heart starts pumping faster and harder, your breathing rate picks up, you start to sweat, and your bowels may try to empty out as your body shifts its focus from your gut to the muscles in your arms and legs.

Now, in the context of a relationship, the "danger" comes from a few places. As mentioned earlier, you've got the evolutionary danger of being isolated, rejected, and cut off—humans are wired to be connected and interdependent, and being rejected or cast out is potentially dangerous. (Interestingly, social connectedness is so important to our survival that the pain of social rejection shares a common neural network with physical pain—a broken heart and a broken bone are, to the brain, both "real" pain.) But you also have all the subconscious filters that you have developed throughout your life and all the other stresses you may be under.

So, after the amygdala makes its assessment, you add in the filters through which you assess a relationship "threat," the filters you built up by your earliest experiences of attachment. And then you throw in all the relationship experiences you've had since then—especially the more emotionally loaded ones, stored in implicit memory, without time stamps. And finally, as if that all weren't enough, you douse the whole pile with in-the-moment, below-awareness physical stressors—running for and missing the train, sitting in a crowded, noisy restaurant, feeling overworked and underslept.

With all of this going on before you even kick it up to conscious awareness, your wiring and filters can lead you to create quite a mess. An unwelcome comment, for example, might draw an immediate "What the hell did you mean by *THAT?*"

There's More to a Relationship Than Fight or Flight

Earlier, you briefly met your autonomic nervous system. Remember that one of its branches, the sympathetic branch, can be thought of as the accelerator pedal in your body. Michelle's accelerator was chronically floored because of her early-childhood wiring and ongoing stress habit, leaving her feeling seriously overstimulated and ready for protective action—*Should I fight? Flee?* Her parasympathetic branch, the one that allows for rest, relaxation, and repose, was rarely in gear.

The longstanding theory of how our autonomic system helps regulate our reactions to the world has been that the accelerator (sympathetic branch) and the brakes (parasympathetic branch) need to be in balance, to work in smooth alternating fashion, depending on the situation. Basically, in this line of thinking, our challenge is to balance between *vroom!* and *stop.*

That's true as far as it goes—but wait! There's more! Let's take a look at another, newer take, from Stephen Porges, PhD,[1] about our reactions to the stress of life—and the stress of love. It's a very helpful way to think about rewiring your body's self-regulation to help you have better, healthier relationships.

Porges takes our understanding of how we regulate our body beyond the notion of balance between the brakes and the accelerator, adding an approach that's incredibly useful as we think about love, attachment, and relationships. His *polyvagal theory* suggests that we've evolved to have *three circuits* (replacing the idea of just two branches).[2]

The third circuit may have developed evolutionarily, as mammals moved into being more and more dependent upon one another for their survival. It has to do with helping us be *better adapted to creating connection with others.* Just as having opposable thumbs allowed us to open new frontiers in what we could accomplish with our hands, having this third circuit—the *smart vagus* (which we touched on briefly in Chapter 2)—moved us forward in our capacity to have social connectedness. Porges's theory has become increasingly influential in how we think about our nervous system and the evolution of attachment and loving relationships.

So how does this work, with three circuits? Information from the outside world enters through one of those low-down brain parts, your thalamus, where it's immediately sent up to that fidgety alarm button, your amygdala, and other deep-in-the-brain limbic players—all below your conscious awareness, before you can even think about it. This is important: these assessments and reactions happen in the body and are first dealt with in the lower, nonthinking, "unaware" brain—not your "aware" brain. (Remember how quickly your amygdala responds—50 milliseconds—compared to the upper, cortical parts of your brain.) These assessments lead to one of three calls:

- If the incoming information is assessed as an immediate, overwhelming, life-threatening danger, the brakes (the parasympathetic branch) get slammed on, and the body immobilizes—shuts or slows way down, basically freezing or "playing dead" to protect itself. If your parasympathetic branch totally dominates, you faint.
- If the incoming information is assessed as a danger that isn't overwhelmingly life-threatening, the sympathetic branch, a.k.a. the accelerator, gets the body to mobilize in response to the threat—the all-too-familiar "fight-or-flight" response—which is also a way that the body tries to protect itself.
- If the assessment is that the incoming information indicates things are safe, the third circuit (your smart vagus) essentially "turns down the volume" of the fight-flight response and allows social engagement to happen: a calm state is created that supports being connected with others. Being in this state allows for better health, growth, and communication.

In either of the first two scenarios, you get taken to an extreme—completely "on" or completely "off." (By the way, your ability to communicate—to listen, or to engage your own speech centers—in either of these states is lousy.) The third scenario is different from just the basic "on/off" switch of the other branches of your autonomic system. Think of your smart vagus as a sort of volume control, which has greater finesse than just "vroom" or "stop." I also like to think of it as a third, more "advanced" method of self-preservation, and it would make sense that this would be hardwired into our bodies just like the first two, if only for survival and evolutionary purposes.

Smart Vagus

The smart vagus is a well-insulated, fast-running nerve that not only calms down the heart and lungs, but also has a role to play in perceiving the sound of other people's voices (that's where the middle-ear muscles come in, in case you've been wondering) and their facial expressions. It activates when we perceive (again, at a level below our awareness) a softening of the facial muscles in others and a relaxation in their tone of voice—in other words, when our body senses that it's safe to be connected. When the smart vagus is "on," we have a greater capacity to really listen, in a tuned-in way, to others, and to send them "it's safe to connect with me" signals as well.

So what you want to be able to create in your body and your brain for better relationships is a sense of greater safety—that way, fight, flight, and playing dead aren't your only choices when things get stressful between you and your significant other.

When your limbic system (including your amygdala and its cohorts) and your sympathetic system aren't acting like a band of lone vigilantes sounding the alarm at every turn, your smart vagus can have greater influence more often. As a result, you're more frequently able to recognize (and even create) a zone of safety and comfort, and you're more primed to engage in connection and attachment. So here's how the smart vagus does its job.

When your body's regulation of its basic state of affairs—heart rate, breathing, stress-hormone levels, and so on—allows you to feel safer more of the time, you can be active and alert, in balance with feelings of calmness and receptivity, and better at social engagement—that is, being in relationship.

This can work in sort of self-perpetuating loops: In the "good" loop, your body perceives safety, and your smart vagus does its warm-and-fuzzy thing. Your face softens, your voice is more relaxed, and the person you're with perceives safety, too—so his face softens, his voice relaxes, and then it feeds back to you, back and forth between the two of you. Good to go.

If, instead, the "not-so-good" loop is in play, you move through the world with an overall sense that there's a lack of safety: Your body and brain are torqued to be hyper-sensitive to threat, and so your smart vagus never gets to come out and play. This is what was happening in Michelle's life. And since you're far less likely to perceive safety, your face is tight, your muscles are tense, your voice is edgy, and you're going to have a much harder time promoting a sense of safety in the person you're sitting with. They respond (as you can—and do—imagine) with matching guardedness and discomfort. And so on, like flinging rotten tomatoes back and forth. Good times? Not.

So what does it take to have that increased perception of safety in your body, and to keep you from being under the rule of those panicky vigilantes—even as the inevitable stress of relationships hits you? How do you get your smart vagus to come to your assistance and help you connect?

You need to be able to reliably hit a "pause" button, so you can call upon more of your brain than just your limbic vigilantes, evaluate the threat more accurately, and decide more mindfully how your body might need to respond.

Junction-Box Hero

Okay, so your brain's assessment of danger—via your heart rate, gut tightening, and so on—influences your feelings and reactions. And, it runs both ways: your emotions and reactions influence your heart rate, gut, and so on. Either way, you can end up in a big mess if this flow of information isn't regulated in some integrated way.

Wouldn't it be great if there were some kind of junction box, a sort of centrally important hub involved in this flow of bodily information?

Then we could just, y'know, rewire that, right?

Yes. That junction box would be your insula. The insula is sort of sitting in the middle of all the action.

In the front part (anterior) of the insula, your body states and sensations are "colored in" as social emotions. A taste on your tongue of something rancid travels along the neural pathways to your anterior insula and you feel the social emotion of "disgust." Your partner touches you sensuously and the anterior insula's take on it is "delight."

Experiments in which brain images are taken while the brain is emotionally "in action" have shown that the insula has an important role in not only the perception of pain, changes in heart rate, and other bodily experiences, but also the experience of a number of basic emotions, including anger, fear, happiness, and sadness.

Body sensations + body regulation + emotions, all getting it on together, leads us to . . .

Better Sex

Remember how Michelle and Rob ended up just "going through the motions" during sex? If their body regulation had been more up to speed, things could have gone much, much better. Here's a list of some of the things that the parts of the brain involved in body regulation—the limbic brain, the insula, and so on—have a hand in (so to speak) when it comes to sex.

If you're worried—*Am I as good as her ex-boyfriend? Is he looking at my fat thighs? Is this a slutty thing to do?*—your alarm-button amygdala gets busy. And guess what? When those alarms sound, your body gets the message to constrict blood vessels, reducing blood flow everywhere except for the body parts you need to fight or run. As you might guess, your genitals are not part of that "needed for flight" package. Erections for men and vaginal engorgement for women go bye-bye.

If, going in the other direction, the activity in your anterior insula is online, helping with regulation, body sensation, and emotions, you're better able to feel all the fantastic bodily sensations and changes that are part of a complete sexual experience, in ways that can seem magnified compared to the way you've been feeling them if you've been underutilizing your insula.

Last but not least, there is a study out of Dartmouth that found a correlation between activation of the insula and the quality of orgasm in women.[3] Just in case you were interested in that.

Okay, then. Your insula seems like an excellent place to focus on regulating your body's power (or abuse thereof) in driving your feelings and reactions in relationships.

How do you rewire your insula and your smart vagus for good (instead of crummy) relationships?

I'm so glad you asked.

Meditation, Your Insula, and Your Smart Vagus

You know from the first two chapters that the more you experience or practice something, the more your brain commits resources to creating new neural connections and even new neurons in response to that experience.

Let's go back to Michelle, for example: The things she'd been practicing and experiencing the most when it came to relationships were the perception of danger, her body's prolonged response to stress, and negative thinking. That made her body and brain more likely to continue on those pathways, making those neural highways even wider and faster.

Now, take a look at this: In 2005, Sara Lazar, PhD, and her colleagues at Harvard looked at the brains of mindfulness meditators and compared them to the brains of people who did not meditate.

The biggest difference between the groups? The brains of the meditators had anterior insulae that were significantly thicker than those of the folks who did not meditate.[4]

Another study, conducted in 2007 at the University of Giessen in Germany, used different brain-measurement methods, again comparing the brains of experienced mindfulness meditation practitioners to those of nonmeditators. That study *also* found that the meditators' brains had thicker anterior insulae.[5]

And, as one of the first studies to start from scratch—to show that the differences in the brain found in mindfulness meditators aren't preexisting in people who choose to meditate or become monks—a 2011 study focused on people who had never meditated before. These folks began meditating for the study, and after eight weeks of meditation practice, changes were found in the regions of their brains involved in "learning and memory processes, emotion regulation, self-referential processing, and perspective taking"[6] (seeing things from another's point of view).

The brains of meditators, through their repeated practice, seem to develop a richer, thicker pathway going up from the body to the limbic brain and through the insula (part of that pathway, by the way, is your smart vagus), leading them to perceive information more accurately. Continuing on up the pathway, the insula seems to be in a better-connected, plumper position for sending the information to the higher-level brain—a much less knee-jerk way of figuring out your response than just letting your limbic brain run the show. Now you've got a better-considered decision on how to respond, and that travels back down through your insula. Your limbic brain gets soothing messages, your stress chemicals stop spewing, and your smart vagus does its "calm down and connect" thing.

What Does This Look Like in the Real World?

After Michelle learned about all of this in her work with me, she started practicing mindfulness meditation.

By meditating nearly every day, Michelle was giving herself almost daily experiences of being calm in her body, instead of stressed. This was new for Michelle, and because the brain seems to respond in a big way to novel experiences, it's reasonable to assume that her brain promptly began laying down new pathways as if her life depended on it (which in a way it does—if you're not good at learning and adapting to new situations, your ability to survive in an ever-changing world gets weaker and weaker).

Michelle's brain probably did the same thing that the brains of meditators in the research studies did: grew more and faster connections in the insula and built a better, faster pathway between the limbic brain and the more circumspect higher brain areas. I suspect her smart vagus came out to play more often as well.

One thing that happened during each of Michelle's daily meditation sessions was that her breathing, because she'd bring her awareness to it, was slower and more even. That also made her heart beat more slowly and evenly. All of this body-based information got sent up to the limbic brain. It was a message of safety, and her brain (through her parasympathetic branch and her smart vagus) cooperated in calming things down even more deeply in her body.

What else was going on each time Michelle meditated? Before you read the list below, remember this: the more experience you have of something, the more your brain builds pathways to support taking that route more often and more automatically ("what fires together, wires together").

- She was more consciously aware of her body—its state, her physical sensations—while calm. She got to experience her body as something more than just a high-strung, stressed-out vessel.
- She was repeatedly bringing her awareness back to the moment, the here and now, giving herself—and her brain—more experience with having her perceptions tuned in to what was happening now, rather than

imagining what might happen next or dwelling on what had happened before.

- She was experiencing her emotions—sometimes boredom, anxiety, or sadness, and also sometimes pleasure or joy—without immediately reacting to them. She was practicing simply being aware of them, as she'd be aware of a rainstorm that came in, passed overhead, and then moved out. She experienced what it was like to have feelings and not be hijacked by them.
- When her mind repeatedly wandered off (as it is meant to do), she simply and gently exercised her ability to notice that that had happened, and then brought it back to the present moment. She was creating the habit of being kind to herself when her mind wandered off (replacing the habit of scolding herself when she made a "mistake") and simply and gently getting back on track.

Michelle meditated for only about five minutes at a time at first, but she did it just about every day. After a couple of weeks, she found that she was meditating longer, without trying, and without even being aware of it—what felt like 5 minutes frequently turned out to be 20. She noticed that she'd started to feel less uptight at work and less reactive to her boss's rants. Her shoulders didn't hurt as much. Her boyfriend, Rob, noticed that she didn't jump on him for every minor infraction. Michelle in turn noticed that Rob was more responsive to her, even spontaneously doing thoughtful things for her that she used to have to pester him for. It was feeling nicer to be with him—her body was more relaxed, she was having fewer "date headaches," and she looked forward to their time together more.

Hmm.

So she began to meditate for slightly longer periods, about 30 minutes, just about every day.

Another couple of weeks passed, and she realized that she hadn't had to take antacids, which had been an almost daily staple. She didn't catch the cold that was going around the office. And—she was embarrassed to admit this, even to herself—she was enjoying sex more than she ever had before. Her body wasn't fighting everything anymore.

She found that her habit of running "scripts" in her head of potential future arguments wasn't happening as much; she would notice if she was "out in the future," and she could gently bring herself back to the here and now.

She was noticing little good things more—like when she consciously noted to herself how sweet her neighbor's new puppy was—and noticing and appreciating her experience of joy.

She was scowling less and smiling more, and more people smiled back.

A friend asked if Michelle had changed her eye makeup, because her eyes looked softer and prettier. (Hmm, maybe "a smart vagus is a woman's best cosmetic"?[7])

Even when she did have an argument with Rob, Michelle didn't feel overrun by her internal panicky scramble to defend herself. She didn't fly off the handle or start itching to storm out. Her body didn't tighten up as much, she didn't feel that familiar reddening in her face, and her expression didn't get so hard and fierce. Her voice didn't get tight and screechy, and she didn't burst into tears. If she did start to get physically reactive, she noticed it before it galloped away with her, and she was better able to calm her body back down—on the fly, even in the middle of an argument. When Rob looked like he was getting irritable, Michelle didn't shut down like she used to. Having learned to recognize—in the moment—when her body was starting to veer into alarm mode, and using mindfulness to make her better and faster at calming her nervous system's reactivity, Michelle could regulate her body's responses and keep them from short-circuiting and leaving her in the dark.

As a result, she became better able to find other, more productive ways to respond, and often de-escalate the situation for both of them, not by avoiding or squashing the conflict, but by having the capacity to tolerate working things through.

Now that you understand more about how regulating your body's responses to others can help you create better connections in your romantic relationships, let's get to work on learning how to practice mindfulness meditation so you can start beefing up those essential pathways.

All of the meditation practices in this book are based on the basic mindfulness meditation outlined below. I recommend that you practice this introductory meditation first, at least a few times, once a day (or more, if you'd like). Then, when you feel ready, you can expand your meditation repertoire to include the others in the book. Whenever you like, during the other meditations, or as a refresher, you can always return to this basic practice.

I also like to remind people who are new to meditation, or returning to it after not practicing for some time, that you might feel a bit awkward, trying to get it right or fumbling with the timing—that's the normal process of learning to meditate. As much as possible, be kind to yourself, if for no other reason than to keep your limbic brain from sounding the alarm in response to potential (or actual) scolding.

Along those same lines, when I say "practice" to a lot of my patients, they link it to ideas like "practice makes perfect," and then get tangled in their self-talk—that if they don't do their meditation practice perfectly, it's not worthwhile, or *they're* not worthwhile.

To all of you perfectionists out there—and, on a daily basis, to myself—I say: How about "practice makes progress" instead?

GETTING STARTED: BASIC MINDFULNESS MEDITATION INSTRUCTIONS

If you've never meditated before (or even if you have), you may have some idea that meditation requires being able to sit on the floor with your legs crossed, in a perfectly constructed, perfectly peaceful room, gentle sunlight streaming in while the faint hint of incense wafts over you and the warmth of a candle imperceptibly finds your serenely closed eyes, with your mind completely still.

Gaaaahhh—no wonder so many people think they can't meditate! Who can achieve that?

Let's try again—this time, with equal doses of reality and compassion.

First, I heartily recommend that you read all the way through the instructions and notes before you actually start.

And second, know that while meditators in glossy magazine ads always look quiescently blissed out, meditation isn't always pleasurable. Walking around as most of us do, with lots of stress, has our bodies pumping out stress hormones much of the time. Those find their way into special receptors in your brain, and they basically make you want to seek pleasure—and seek it quickly. The brain is jonesing for a quick squirt of dopamine—sometimes referred to as the "feel-good neurotransmitter," even though it does many other things—and impels you to do something to provide this, such as eat some ice cream or look to see if a new e-mail has arrived. While this will make you feel better *now,* it turns out that it's not good for long-term well-being. So keep in mind that even if your meditation practice doesn't feel good in a given moment, or if your brain is telling you to go do something else quicker and/or "more pleasurable," know that by practicing, you're training your brain to deal with stress more effectively, eliminating much of the *stress—craving pleasure—indulging—stress* cycle in which we so often get trapped.

1. **To begin, just sit down somewhere.** That's all. The rest of this step, in all of its multi-bulleted glory, is to make it a little easier for your sitting* to support you in your meditation, and to put you at ease if you feel more comfortable with detailed instructions.

    - You can sit on a chair. I find it best to choose one that has some cushioning on the seat. It'll be easiest if the height of the seat allows your feet to be comfortably planted on the floor (about a foot apart) and lets your thighs be parallel to the floor (hips at about the same level as knees).

---

*While most people find sitting to be the best position for meditation, you don't have to actually be in a sitting position. You can find more about different positions in the "Resource" section.

- If your chair has a back, sit forward far enough so that you won't find yourself leaning on it unless you need to. (If you do need to have that support, by all means, use it.) The idea is for your body to be able to keep itself upright with ease, a sort of natural balance. Sitting without a chair back to lean on also allows you to know when you're getting drowsy or distracted. I've been known to "come back" to my meditation after realizing with a start that I was about to pitch forward out of my chair and onto my face. (Go ahead and laugh —I did!)
- Find a comfortable place for your hands to rest. Some people like to have their hands in the crook of their lap, resting like two spoons facing their belly. Others like to have their palms on their thighs.
- Your eyes can be slightly open with a "soft focus" (kind of fuzzy-eyed), or closed. If you have your eyes open, you might find it helpful to aim your gaze slightly downward
- Sit with your back straight, but not rigid. It's sometimes helpful to imagine a gentle, elastic string attached to the crown of your head, softly lengthening your spine and neck, with your shoulders able to hang loosely. Perhaps lower your chin slightly until your head feels comfortably placed. Try to remember that this is about ease, not about stretching or pushing, and that being kind to yourself is part of the practice.

2. **Now, just breathe**. Really. Just let the natural rhythm of your breath, whatever it is, lead you; there's no need to force it or change it in any way. Your only task right now is to bring your awareness to the sensations of breathing—the slight tickle of the air just under your nose as you breathe in. The coolness of the air as it enters your nostrils. Feeling the air as it passes down your windpipe. The movement of your chest and belly as your lungs expand, then contract. Bring your awareness to any one, or more, of these sensations (or any others you become aware of) as you breathe in and out.

3. **Did your mind immediately wander? Good!** With kindness and gentleness, simply bring it back. Just like a puppy that's naturally curious, your mind is meant to wander off, get distracted, and so on. So, when it does, gently and lovingly bring it back to the sensations of your breath, just as you'd bring that soft, sweet puppy back to you. Like scolding a puppy, angrily chastising your mind for wandering off is going to make it less likely to want to be close to you (or maybe even make it pee on the floor, poor thing).

   The busier your brain is, the more opportunities you have to notice that your mind has wandered and to gently and lovingly bring it back. (Those actions—the noticing and bringing back—are what neuroscientists like Richard Davidson, PhD, believe may be the brain-wiring "reps," like the repeated biceps curls a weightlifter does to build muscle.)

4. **That's all there is to it**—that's the basic form of how you practice mindfulness meditation. Whenever you're done, gently open your eyes and slowly reenter your day. Start with just a few minutes of practice and invite yourself to gradually increase your practice over time.

One more important note before you move into meditation—and as a good reminder all along the way: please be gentle with yourself. Sometimes, while meditating, things might come into awareness that we otherwise avoid, or that are particularly difficult, such as an old emotional wound or something big that we need to change in our lives. In this case, it may be helpful to stop the meditation and get some support, such as psychotherapy, to help you deal with the issues. I've included some suggestions and resources later in the book.

CHAPTER 4

Circuit Breakers to Prevent Overheating

Fear Modulation

Fear. If I were perfectly concise and accurate, that would be the sum total of my response to the question "What do you specialize in as a psychotherapist?"

Because, when you get right down to it, that's what we're all dealing with, in one way or another. Fear, fear *of* fear, fear of conflict, fear of being alone, fear of getting too close, fear of failure, fear of success, fear of dying, fear of really living . . .

Now that you've started to get some traction on body regulation, the next big source of energy to contend with is fear. It's our most fundamental (and arguably most powerful) emotion, so it's the first one to keep an eye on and learn to modulate.

Fear and Loving: Rebecca

"I'm just so stuck in this relationship. I know it's over, I know I need to end it, but I just can't seem to do it. I need to figure out why I won't leave, so I can move on."

In front of me sat Rebecca: smart, fit, successful . . . and *very* stuck.

She described her partner of 14 years, Vince, as someone who struggled to make a decent living, had few friends, and "could not care less about trying to understand his issues. He just complains that life is passing him by." Not surprisingly, Rebecca—like most of my patients—had come in on her own since she couldn't get Vince to come in for therapy.

She'd been trying for several years to end things with Vince and to figure out why she wouldn't leave. She'd thought about it long and hard with her very strong higher-reasoning abilities.

What her higher-reasoning abilities overlooked was fear. It was as if her cortex looked around and said, "Fear? We ain't got no fear. We don't need no stinking fear!" To Rebecca, life was best approached by understanding the problem and then finding the solution. Feelings just confused things. Leave 'em by the side of the road.

And, indeed, Rebecca didn't look like someone who lived fearfully. She walked confidently, handled the big responsibilities of her international job well, and reveled in high-risk recreational pursuits. She'd enjoyed getting her pilot's license, trekking the mountains of Himalaya, spelunking in South America, and scuba diving on the Great Barrier Reef—shark city.

Hang gliding? No problem.

Hanging on to herself in a relationship? Not so much.

Rebecca described herself as having grown up in "a pretty typical rural American family." Her parents were of the "emotions are for sissies" variety, with little expressed warmth. Life was about doing your best and making do. The only exceptions to the no-emotions rule were her father's anger and her mother's distancing disappointment—both of which came out by the truckload whenever Rebecca or her siblings brought home anything less than top-level achievement.

"Nobody ever talked about disowning us," Rebecca said, "but there was a way that we always felt like we were one phone call away from being packed up and sent off to distant relatives."

When Rebecca was 15, her 27-year-old brother committed suicide. "Once the funeral was over, my parents just never talked about him anymore. It was like he'd just—poof—disappeared, or never even existed." Her guess was that they'd felt ashamed of her brother's action and maybe even angry at him for bringing shame upon the family—but that there was "no way they could've ever looked inside themselves" for how they might have contributed to his pain. She remembers that she simply felt a gaping black hole when her brother died.

When Rebecca was 18 and away at college, she met—and not long after, moved in with—a guy who, as she saw him in retrospect, "was my dad, minus the anger."

She said she'd known she loved him by the feelings she'd had when he was around, or whenever he called: "It was like instead of having a black hole, I was plugged into a high-voltage socket—not because he was a live wire!" she joked. "But because he'd pay attention to me, even the tiniest bit. Compared to my family, it was like rocket fuel!"

As we'll see, rocket fuel is not really the elixir of love.

Everything You Never Wanted to Know about Fear, Because You Were Afraid to Ask

Before we even get to the first item on the list of "important things to know about fear," here's another important little tidbit: *fear is the reason you're reading this book.*

We figure out how to modulate our fear response (for better or worse) in our earliest attachments, and that method—in our nervous system and in our behavior—sticks with us and makes itself known throughout our adult relationships, unless we install some circuit breakers.

Now, on to that list of important things to know.

Important Thing Number One: Fear isn't about "now"—it's about anticipating the future pain/hurt you might experience, or even that you are definitely going to experience—but you're not experiencing right now. In this moment, you're okay.

Take a moment to imagine you're on the African plains. Suddenly, you see a lion running across the veld toward you. Fear! But—in that moment: Are you okay? Actually, you are. You're not hurt, you're not dead, in that moment. You're anticipating what might happen, but in that moment, you're actually fine. How about now that you're running, and the lion is catching up? Fear, definitely: What if (future) he catches you? Maybe you will be (future) maimed, or worse, but—in this moment, while you're running—you're okay. Until that angry lion actually catches you, until the thing that you're worried about actually happens, you're okay.

Checking in like that, moment to moment, when you're anxious or afraid, can be very helpful. It's a bit like those advertisements for the mobile phone service, "Can you hear me now? Good." Am I okay now? Good.

Important Thing Number Two: Fear and anger are intimately related. A few thoughts about anger: At its core, anger is about unmet needs. (Minor example: if I get angry at the person who cut me off in traffic this morning, the unmet need was to be able to reasonably assume that I'm not going to get my car totaled on the way to work.) What we're really mad about is based in our fear that our needs aren't going to be met—that we're going to experience pain or hurt or violation, be it of our trust or of our safety. So, modulating fear gets you benefits in dealing with anger as well. Good stuff.

Important Thing Number Three: Hiding from our fear gets in the way. We often distract ourselves from fear by busying or girding ourselves with anger, numbness, busyness, or detachment. Those are defensive (or sometimes offensive) maneuvers. As you're able to develop increased mindfulness and tune in to the fear, you're more likely to discover the key to the lock: being compassionately curious about what the fear is, underneath those defenses, often reveals the genuine treasure hidden beneath.

If you acknowledge your fear, you can learn how to deal with it (and to relate to others around you) in a much more effective, healthy way. It's like being able to understand why a baby is crying—if you can calm yourself down long enough to tune in, you'll be able to know that the baby is hungry or overtired, and from there, you can be a more effective caregiver.

Important Thing Number Four: Fear stresses the body—including your brain. We do need some fear to boost our chances of survival. Too much, though, shuts down the higher centers of your brain—the ones you need for learning and thinking clearly and problem solving. Not a good place to hang out for very long. Having some fear is necessary—it's what makes you look both ways before crossing the street—but too much and you end up "dead" in another way.

Feeding the Fear

Imagine that you're in a cage. In the cage with you is a hungry tiger.[1] Let's name that snarling, demanding beast your "anxiety tiger." The tiger starts pacing over to you, and, since you want to keep it from eating you, you throw it some meat. Whew. Problem averted.

But you're still in the cage. And after a while, the tiger gets hungry again. He's got you trained now—anxiety tiger starts growling, and you feed it some meat—some of your internal resources, some of your vitality.

More tiger-advances. More meat-tossing. You could keep—and probably have kept—this up for a loooooong time. It's what many of us do in response to fear and anxiety, and it costs us dearly.

How about getting out of the cage? Instead of throwing meat to the anxiety tiger over and over again—in other words, instead of giving in to the demands of your fears and anxieties—what if you could get better at noticing when your anxiety tiger is starting to pace, decide not to get in the pattern of throwing meat to it again, open the door to the cage, and walk out?

That would be a mindful approach, eh?

Practicing mindfulness helps you calm the anxiety tiger. It helps you notice when the tiger starts to snarl, recognize when you're in the cage with it again, and decide not to feed it with your old habits.

Being afraid and interpreting the world (especially the world of relationships) from an anxious, fearful perspective might seemingly keep you safe, might keep the tiger in the cage with you from eating you, but it costs you in many ways, and it keeps you a meat-tossing prisoner of your own anxiety.

The Unthought Known Rides Again

Your amygdala—and the fear response it generates—is helpful to your survival in large part because it never forgets potential dangers. But remember that your amygdala stores "fear" memories without any reference to when the fearful event occurred—so when it's called up from storage, you experience the fear as "here and now," whether that's true or not. It's an unconscious, undated, never-expiring memory whose job it is to generalize that fear as broadly and as frequently as possible, to keep you as "safe" as possible. These are the implicit memories we've discussed previously.

In the realm of relationships, that means that any fearful or painful or otherwise potentially unsafe memories of long-ago relationship experiences are at the ready to try to "help" you avoid being hurt today. Those memories are in there, waiting for anything even remotely similar to trigger them, below your awareness.

You can imagine this going on for Rebecca—she could live in a lousy relationship and endure its emptiness for 14 years, because whenever there was a chance of being alone—recalling her childhood fear of being a phone call away from being an orphan—her amygdala (followed by a flood of neurochemicals) sounded the alarm. So even in the present, as a full-grown, highly competent adult, Rebecca's "thinking" brain (her cortex) didn't even know how much it was getting pushed around by this old, outdated news, those old feeling-memories. It just . . . was. So Rebecca just . . . stayed.

Eventually, her brain came to assume the following line of "reasoning" (in quotes because, as you'll see, it's pretty flawed): *I haven't left Vince for 14 stultifying years because I might die if I'm alone. I'm alive, which must be because I've stayed with Vince. So I'd better stay.*

And it wasn't as if Rebecca's friends hadn't tried to convince her to leave Vince. Her amygdala just managed to manufacture more compelling neurochemical, unconscious, old-fear arguments in favor of staying.

I think one of the best labels for this kind of emotional memory is from Christopher Bollas, PhD. He called it the "unthought known." It's incredibly powerful, because self-preservation (as assessed by the amygdala) is always first and foremost in your nervous system.

For Rebecca, her emotional memory's "theory" was that staying put and maintaining an attachment at all costs was the best course of action. The unmodulated, untagged fear generated by her amygdala couldn't see it any other way, and in effect it put its hands over the eyes of the rest of her brain to prevent the rest of Rebecca from seeing it any other way either.

Which takes us to a quote from Albert Einstein: "Whether you can observe a thing or not depends on the theory which you use. It is the theory which decides what can be observed."[2]

In this case, it's your amygdala's fear-based theory that decides. Unless, of course, you have ways to modulate that fear, so you won't be ruled by it.

And hey, whaddaya know? *There are healthy circuit breakers for fear.*

Do-It-Yourself Healthy Circuit Breakers for Fear

As you're certainly aware by now, fear is a many-splendored thing. It keeps you vigilant for potential danger, keeps you running in the face of present danger—good things for survival—but if it doesn't dissipate, it contributes to inflammation, heart disease, lousy immunity, ulcers, you name it, including the relationship-busting reactions we've been talking about. Fear can be acute, or it can be chronic; it can protect you, and it can wreck you. So maybe it'll come as no surprise that the fear circuit breakers listed below come in different varieties as well—some are quick and in-the-moment, and others involve creating longer-term habits through mindfulness meditation that rewire your response and recovery over time. Having a wide array of circuit breakers integrated into your daily life will serve you well.

Circuit Breaker #1: Delivering GABA to the Amygdala: You know those old cowboy movies where someone's been bitten by a rattlesnake and there's a race against time to find some anti-venom—another substance that counteracts the venom's deadly effect on the body?

In the case of the overreactive amygdala, the antivenom is GABA (gamma-aminobutyric acid). You learned a little about GABA before, when we talked about emotional regulation. In the adult human brain, GABA acts as an *inhibitory neurotransmitter*—you can think of it as a chemical override switch, which, if you hit it, turns the alarm button off.

Your OMPFC (orbitomedial prefrontal cortex) has a GABA delivery system at the ready, with especially strong projections (think of them as delivering arms) going to the amygdala. Building more of those projections from the OMPFC to the amygdala, and delivering more soothing, inhibitory GABA, means you're building in a circuit breaker. Getting better at bringing your prefrontal cortex online—that is, being more aware of your thoughts and experiences in the moment—makes the prefrontal cortex an even better circuit breaker, because then it knows when to deliver the goods—the GABA—to calm your amygdala.

Circuit Breaker #2: Upping Your Oxytocin: Oxytocin is the neurotransmitter often referred to as the "cuddle hormone" because of its role in social bonding and attachment.

Oxytocin serves as an excellent circuit breaker for two reasons: First, like GABA, it seems to have an inhibitory effect on your amygdala's response to fear. Second, it seems to encourage the growth of those projections from the OMPFC to the amygdala that deliver GABA.

When and where does your brain produce oxytocin? In a small part of your limbic system called (buckle up) the *paraventricular nucleus of the hypothalamus* (sometimes called the PVN or PVH). It's a small cluster within your hypothalamus—one of many. And it's basically *the* source of oxytocin in your brain. That's the "where."

The "when" about oxytocin production provides an important clue to how you can increase your oxytocin action: The hypothalamus sends out more oxytocin when you feel calm and safe in the presence of another—or even, it seems, if you simply think of someone with whom you feel safe. It also sends out more when you're hugging (especially, according to some, when that hug presses snugly and safely against your chest and belly).

So you have the potential to increase your own oxytocin output by simply thinking of someone with whom you feel safe and loved, or maybe by being safely touched on your chest and belly.

Circuit Breaker #3: Activating the Parasympathetic Branch of Your Autonomic Nervous System: In the analogy used before, the sympathetic branch of your nervous system is the gas pedal—the thing that makes you zoom into fighting or fleeing. The parasympathetic branch, in contrast, can be thought of as the brake pedal—its activation brings about a state of relaxing, restoring, and repairing, which is the opposite of the fear response. It's really much more than a "stop" mechanism, though—when you're in a state that's shifted toward the parasympathetic branch, not only does your body have the opportunity to recover, but you're also in the state of mind needed for playing, creating, and daydreaming. This is often when thoughts and ideas and feelings that were previously not "connected" come together and make sense, giving you clearer insight.

Here's a great opportunity to see how mindfulness benefits complement and support one another: Being aware of what's going on in your body, as you started to practice in Chapter 3, helps you know when your fear response is starting to rev up. Then, applying the simple things on the list below will help your autonomic nervous system switch from the accelerator to the brakes, shifting toward a more balanced state and allowing your parasympathetic branch to open things up. You can do any or all of the things on this list any time you notice that your body is in need of some regulation or your fear is in need of some modulation. You'll also be practicing them in the mindfulness exercise at the end of this chapter.

- **Breathe a bit more slowly, a bit more deeply.** This sends the message, from your lungs and your heart, that things aren't dangerous "out there" in the world. Your vagus nerve carries that message up to your brain stem, and the cascade of chemicals that were stimulating your body's fear response is turned off.
- **Relax your tongue.** Relaxing your tongue also sends feedback through the vagus nerve that everything is okay, getting the parasympathetic nervous system working to soothe you.
- **Open your mouth slightly.** Again, a relaxed jaw gets the message to your brain that it can relax, too, via the vagus nerve.
- **Imagine increased warmth in your hands.** When you're under threat or stressed, your sympathetic nervous system acts to direct blood flow to where you're likely to need it most if you're going to need to run for your life or fight—that's into the big muscles in your body, like your legs. It directs blood flow away from less important areas, like your hands and fingers.

> By imagining warmth (which accompanies increased blood flow) in your hands, you're sending yet another signal to your sympathetic nervous system to take it easy and let the parasympathetic branch set the more relaxed tone. Biofeedback and hypnosis techniques for relaxation, pain management, and stress reduction very often utilize hand warming for this reason.

Circuit Breaker #4: Shifting from a Right-Brain (Avoid) Mode to the Left (Approach): You already know something about this idea from our earlier explorations of right-and-left-hemisphere integration. You get substantial relationship benefits from balancing your often dominant right hemisphere with your left hemisphere, making you more receptive and less likely to fight or flee. You also already know, from our discussion in Chapter 2, that we're all prone to walking around with a right-hemisphere bias—leading us to tilt toward negative moods, fear, and so on. As a budding mindfulness meditator, though, your brain activity is shifting toward greater left-hemisphere activation. Shifting away from letting your right brain rule means shifting away from letting fear run your life—and your relationships.

Circuit Breaker #5: Making the Most of Your Anterior Cingulate Cortex: In what I think may be one of the top ten best uses of pop culture in the explanation of neuroscience, Steven Schlozman, MD, of Harvard University, uses zombies to help explain the importance of the anterior cingulate cortex in modulating fear. As you've already seen, the anterior cingulate cortex, together with the insula, acts a sort of balancing middleman between the amygdala and the frontal cortex. Schlozman was watching the classic horror film *Night of the Living Dead,* and, being a neuroscientist, he noticed that the zombies "had a whole lot of amygdala going on . . . Then there's an intermediary part of the brain, the anterior cingulate cortex, which helps to modulate communications between higher and lower brain. And I figured that probably wasn't working so good [in the zombie's brains], because you figure in normal humans, if that lower brain gets too loud, the anterior cingulate cortex helps to modulate it so the frontal lobe can process it in time. But zombies don't process things that well."[3]

Yup. Zombies are driven by their amygdalas, without an ACC to help modulate their fear (or their anger and aggression, which as you learned earlier, are so closely related that we often can't tell them apart—if you're in doubt, scare a crocodile sometime and see what happens). So they, um, eat people.

Makes you want to beef up your own ACC, yes? Well, neuroscientists are starting to show that mindfulness practice—in as little as three hours total—seems to increase ACC activity in ways that improve emotional regulation. In as little as 11 total hours of mindfulness practice, one set of researchers showed that there were structural changes in an important neural pathway connecting the ACC to other structures[4]—again, related to improved emotional regulation.

Circuit Breaker #6: Increasing the Integration of Your Brain: You know by now that the better integrated your brain is, from top to bottom and from side to side, the better your overall well-being. Making sure that your lower-right limbic system isn't driving the bus out there all on its own—without higher brain areas or the left side to help—is key. Bringing more of your brain into the picture means that the communication pathway is a little bit longer. This is a good thing, because it gives the rest of your brain a little more time to process what's going on and come up with a broader range of possible ways to respond. You don't just make a mad dash from your limbic brain's alarmist judgment straight to having a reaction. Your whole brain has a bit of time to get a tad more grounded and to riffle through the card deck of options. In particular, you have the time for your prefrontal cortex (PFC) to get on board and act as a more reasonable (literally, as in *reasoning*) guide.

It's like taking the longer, more scenic route home to give yourself time and space to sort out the stress of your day, get more balanced, gain some perspective, relax your shoulders, and remember that you love your boyfriend and he loves you, before walking in the door. (Which, by the way, is something I *highly* recommend.)

All of these circuit breakers are already well installed if you've had the experience of healthy, secure, attuned, contingently responsive attachment in childhood.

That little phrase there, "contingently responsive," is an important one. Daniel Siegel gives a great description of it and how it ties together with early childhood attachment: "Attachment at its core is based on parental sensitivity and responsivity to the child's signals, which allow for collaborative parent-child communication. Contingent communication gives rise to secure attachment and is characterized by a collaborative give-and-take of signals between the members of a pair. Contingent communication relies on the alignment of internal experiences, or states of mind, between child and caregiver. This mutually sharing, mutually influencing set of interactions—this emotional attunement or mental state resonance—is the essence of healthy, secure attachment."[5]

By having a caregiver who responds to you in an attuned, contingent way, you (and your brain and your body) learn how to put those circuit breakers into play, and prevent "over-fear," so you don't end up as anxious or avoidant as you might be otherwise.

Whether anxious or avoidant, it is, as you've seen, all about fear.

What's interesting is that we don't necessarily choose our partners based on who will reduce our fear most.

Nope.

In one study, women with an anxious style of attachment were more likely to date men with an avoidant style of attachment—the very guys who were more likely to stir up their anxiety.[6]

In another study, people with an avoidant attachment style were typically more interested in being with anxious-attachment-style partners.[7]

Now, why would we do that to ourselves?

Maybe because we feel safer when we get confirmation of who we think we are, or of our personal attachment theory about how love works. *Status quo.* None of this stretching-yourself stuff when you're in the middle of fear.

Keep in mind where, for example, someone's anxious attachment style (and wiring) began: the earliest (and most familiar) attachment was with someone who showed up inconsistently and in only small amounts. For someone with that history, to be loved is to be anxious, punctuated with the occasional "hit" of the good stuff.

It's a little like a slot machine programmed to keep us there sticking our nickels in—variable-ratio reinforcement, for you behaviorists out there. Hits, or rewards, are received after you've gone through an unpredictable number of anxiety-driven thoughts and behaviors. After 3, 12, 25, or 147 anxious thoughts: *Payoff!* You just never know when you might get a little tiny jackpot. Variable-ratio reinforcement, not incidentally, is the best way to train up a good, solid, hard-to-break addictive behavior. It's part of what makes gambling so addictive.

After a day spent wondering anxiously—*is he going to call, did he get my text, why isn't he responding*—he finally does call, and *whew,* that feels good. And the familiar long-term pattern is reinforced.

Sounds like how Rebecca described her early signs of "love" with Vince.

By the time Rebecca came in to see me, her feelings in the relationship had evolved over its long course from the initially obvious preoccupation and obsessive anxiety into a quieter form: *Does he care about me? Does he love me? Is he going to show up emotionally today/this week/this month/next year?* Again, the addiction trained up by variable-ratio reinforcement is the hardest kind to break. You just never know when you might get another hit, so you hang in there.

Early in the course of our work together, Rebecca started meditating regularly. She had tried meditation before, but she had found it difficult because she was trying to "get it right" and "stop my brain—I just failed miserably!" We talked about how mindfulness isn't about stopping your brain (that would be mind*less*ness), but about noticing what your mind is doing. Rebecca also noted that she'd stopped meditating in part because Vince seemed to feel threatened by it—maybe at some level he knew it was a way for Rebecca to grow in a way that he wouldn't.

Rebecca was also having a hard time accepting what would happen if she "succeeded" at being less afraid of being alone. Her thinking went something like this: If she were no longer afraid of leaving Vince or of being in the black hole, she'd "have to" leave, but she'd then be in that awful black hole. From where she sat, at the beginning of the process, she couldn't convincingly conceive of her "new" self down the road, with less fear, dealing with being alone more easily.

It's like another quote attributed to Einstein: "The significant problems we face cannot be solved at the same level of thinking that created them."

Armed with the neuro-knowledge that meditation could help her brain be less overwhelmed by her fear of the black hole, and that she could make the decision (to stay with Vince or leave) from a less fearful place, she started practicing mindfulness meditation regularly. Rebecca eventually held on to herself long enough to decide to end her unhealthy relationship with Vince.

As we continued our work together, Rebecca and I then got to see, with the next person she dated, how those early stages of anxious attachment played out for her. She met a guy who was unavailable in so many ways it was hard to keep count, but on those rare occasions when he did show up, it was like a drug for Rebecca. She'd forgive all the other avoidant behaviors for that one wonderful call, e-mail, or weekend together.

This time though, it didn't take her 14 years to recognize what she was doing and how familiar it all was. It took a monumental amount of courage for her to unhook from the drug, to stop feeding her anxiety tiger. But she did it. You know it wasn't just about breaking up with the guy; it was about making a radical shift in how she dealt with her fear of being alone. She was doing it.

In less than six months, Rebecca met Ralph. At first, she felt mostly "meh" about Ralph, even though he had all the right things on paper, and then some. She said there just wasn't that "spark." As we talked more about Ralph, I remarked to Rebecca that it sounded as if maybe Ralph was a guy who had the capacity for secure attachment—he wasn't doing the avoidant dance.

Then, in a completely gorgeous "Aha!" and then "Holy Toledo, what am I doing?!" moment, she realized that the spark that was missing was her anxiety and those rare good hits that would punctuate it.

It was a little scary for Rebecca to have someone showing up consistently—but this was a very different kind of fear. Plus, she was now responding to fear in different, healthier ways, with more (and more efficient) circuit breakers in place.

Calming the Surges with the Circuit Breakers

In our work together to help Rebecca modulate her fear in healthier ways, we used a variety of mindfulness practices. (One was "mindful online dating," using one of the dating sites to help her recognize what her body was doing in response to the on-screen personas of potential dates!) She felt that while all of the mindfulness practices were helpful, the meditation below was the one she turned to most often.

It's an adaptation of an excellent meditation by Linda Graham, MFT, a psychotherapist and trainer/consultant who is a longtime student of mindfulness.

The meditation is built around several ideas—many of which can be traced to the healthy circuit breakers described above:

- **Delivering GABA to the amygdala**. This exercise, as a mindfulness meditation, can stimulate the growth of neuronal fibers from the prefrontal cortex down toward the amygdala. And remember that these fibers carry GABA, the neurotransmitter that counteracts the amygdala's fear signals.
- **Upping your oxytocin, part 1**. Being touched by someone with whom you feel safe can stimulate the

hypothalamus to release oxytocin—and how convenient: that could include your own touch. In this exercise you'll be placing one hand on your heart and one on your belly.

- **Upping your oxytocin, part 2.** Evoking mental imagery of a loved one, or of feeling safe and loved, is also an effective way to calm the body and release oxytocin.
- **Activating the parasympathetic branch of your autonomic nervous system.** Your heart and your gut are two areas rich in neural circuits that tell your brain how you're doing—are you safe? Having a supportive, gentle hand on each of those areas helps soothe them, leading to feedback to the brain (via the vagus nerve) that you're okay. You'll also be shifting toward the parasympathetic branch of your autonomic nervous system, through relaxed, natural, slightly deeper breathing, relaxing your tongue, opening your jaw, and imagining warmth flowing into your hands.
- **Shifting from a right-brain (avoid) mode to the left (approach).** By practicing this exercise, you'll be "priming" yourself to feel safe, connected, or loved—lowering your right brain's usual flurry of activity and cultivating more action on the left—which you now understand as a buffer for your body's and brain's fear-based response to subsequent stressors.
- **Making the most of your anterior cingulate cortex.** Mindfulness practice can increase the pathways connecting your ACC to other structures, and contribute to other ways of integrating your middle prefrontal cortex.

Ready to install some circuit breakers?

CIRCUIT BREAKER MEDITATION

First, settle into your body and your breath, as described in the Basic Mindfulness Meditation in Chapter 3.

Invite yourself to move slowly through the meditation exercise, taking your time with each step.

Bring your awareness to your jaw and your mouth. Allow your tongue to relax inside your mouth and let your jaw open slightly. Feel your breath passing easily through your relaxed throat.

When you feel ready, gently place your hand on your heart, in the center of your chest. Place your other hand on your lower belly, below your navel.

Imagine your hands getting warmer, the tiny capillaries and arteries relaxing just a bit to allow warmth to flow into them.

Breathe gently and deeply, imagining the breath going into your heart and your belly. With each breath, invite yourself to also breathe into your heart and your belly any sense of goodness, safety, trust, acceptance, or ease that you're able to bring to mind.

Once that's steady, call to mind a moment of being with someone who loves you unconditionally, someone you feel completely safe with. This may not always be a partner or a parent or a child. Those relationships can be so complex and the feelings can be mixed. It may be, for example, a good friend or a trusted teacher. It may be your therapist, your grandmother, a third-grade teacher, or a beloved pet. Pets are great.

As you remember feeling safe and loved with this person or pet, see if you can feel the feelings and sensations that come up with that memory in your body. Allow yourself to really savor these feelings of warmth, safety, trust, and love in your body.

When that feeling is steady, gently release the image for now and simply bathe in the feeling for 30 seconds or so.

As always, when you're done with your formal practice, gently and gradually bring yourself back into the room and into the stream of daily life.

CHAPTER 5

Installing a Dimmer Switch

Emotional Resilience

Just can't shake the feeling. You had a conversation with your partner this morning, it went badly, and hours later you're still running it through your head (and through your body, as you learned earlier).

This kind of emotional "stuckness" can definitely get in the way of your capacity to be present in your relationships—it keeps grabbing you and pulling you back into the quicksand of painful past experiences.

If only you could wrestle yourself free. You try thinking it over, running the argument through your mind over and over trying to figure it out, but that just seems to leave you more engulfed in the swamp of feelings—maybe anger, maybe worry, maybe sadness. Eventually you seem to get over it, but then something minor, maybe even completely unrelated, happens, and *BAM*—you're right in the emotional fire-swamp again—maybe with your partner, or maybe with someone else who just happens to be in the wrong place at the wrong time. Back and forth, back and forth. Reminds me of a joke:

> A Ferrari and a bicycle pull up at the same stoplight.
>
> The bicyclist asks, "How fast can she go?"
>
> "Over 200 miles an hour."
>
> "Wow!" The bicyclist leans over, looks around inside the car. Sitting back up, he says, "It's fantast—"
>
> Just then, the light turns green, and the Ferrari zooms off.
>
> The Ferrari driver tools along for a bit—and suddenly, whoooooshhhh! The bicycle flies past him in a blur.
>
> "What the—?" So he punches the accelerator. Suddenly, he sees the bicycle hurtling back toward him, and it flies by again. He can't believe it!
>
> "No way," he thinks. He slows down a little, wondering if he might be hallucinating.
>
> Looking in his rearview mirror, he sees the bicyclist coming up fast.
>
> The bicyclist manages to shout as he whips by: "Unhook my suspenders from your side-view mirror!!!"

So keeping your brain from getting flung about by your internal Ferrari of emotion would be a good thing. In Chapters 3 and 4, you started to shift your primitive physical reactions and your fear out of the driver's seat. Now you can turn your attention to other emotional states and, when needed, recover from them more quickly—more mindfully.

Not Mr. Spock

The term *emotional regulation* often confuses people. *Won't I end up feeling kinda blah and boring if my emotions are so . . . regulated?*

Or, *Isn't being able to scream/sob/vent my anger what therapists are always telling us to do?*

Let's be clear: The idea isn't to get rid of your emotions or squash them down. Anger, fear, sadness—in fact, all your emotions—serve important purposes. After all, the emotions that you experience when your limbic system senses danger and punches the accelerator are sometimes literally life-saving! And emotions don't only serve to protect you, they are a vital, necessary part of being a human. They make life—relationships, work, parenting—vibrant and worthwhile. We tend to think of certain emotions as negative, or bad, but it's far more helpful to think of these seemingly negative forces as powerful tools. It's true that they can overwhelm us and fling us about mercilessly (and unconsciously), but if we learn how to keep them from running our lives, the benefits and aliveness of experiencing them are like the difference between living in black and white versus Technicolor.

If all you can experience is the extreme emotion, though—the surge of the engine, unintended collisions, blowing gaskets, or running out of gas—you're missing out on a lot. And if all you try to do is keep it in neutral with your foot on the brake, you're missing even more. I've heard Daniel Goleman, PhD, say it really well—what we're aiming for with emotional resilience: "to stay with the discomfort—to not run toward the hedonic—and to be able to choose a more mindful response. You can hold in awareness the feeling of *wanting to avoid*—you get the strength so that even distressful feelings can remain in awareness without overwhelming you."[1]

So you're neither dodging the emotions nor indulging yourself (or drowning) in them. Once you've faced the emotions and expressed them (to yourself and perhaps to others) mindfully, you'll find that it's much easier to have a rich emotional life without being jammed up, periodically volcanic, or emotionally limp.

As Richard Davidson, PhD, put it, "Negative emotion is one which persists beyond the time it is useful. Regulation means it doesn't persist, and that you can return to baseline."[2] Bingo.

What? Where? How?

What goes on in the brain when it comes to emotional resilience? What changes might we actually be aiming for and bringing about? Here are brief summaries of three recent studies that suggest how the brain works in regard to emotional resilience:

Study Number One: Using the top to regulate the bottom: greater resilience even after the alarm has sounded. A study of our brain's responses while looking at our partner's facial expressions showed that the more activity there is in part of your prefrontal cortex (PFC), the more resilient your emotional state will be after a conflict.[3] The better you are at getting your PFC online, the better you can "bounce back" emotionally. Think of it as having firm but flexible control of the reins on a horse. The PFC is like the reins, and the horse—your emotional state—doesn't veer as far off course, or run amok.

Study Number Two: "Using your words" to soothe your amygdala works better with mindfulness. In another study, people were asked to verbally label faces that showed different emotions. Those who had higher scores on a measure of mindfulness showed more activity in the PFC and better deactivation of the amygdala in response to the faces with "negative" emotions. Basically, their brains were better than nonmeditators' at using language (left hemisphere) to avoid getting caught up in the negative affect they saw. The higher the mindfulness score, the more the PFC was able to "calm" the amygdala.[4]

Study Number Three: Shifting your brain's bias toward the left hemisphere improves mood and resilience. Perhaps most compelling is the work that Davidson's group has done on the ratio of left-to-right prefrontal activity.[5] All of us, at rest, have a sort of baseline ratio between the activity in the two sides of our prefrontal cortex. If you tend to have more activity on the right, Davidson and colleagues found, you're more likely to end up in the grips of negative emotions and stay there longer. (Remember the right-hemisphere bias we talked about before?) Those who are more left-active tend to have more positive emotions—and they tend to recover from negative experiences much more quickly. They have greater resilience. Most of us fall somewhere in the middle of these two types of emotional "set points"—but being able to shift your baseline activity more toward the left, with more positive mood states and greater resilience, sure sounds good to me—for myself, for my patients, and for you.

Because of these studies and others like them, we're going to look at doing two things that are important in increasing emotional resilience: shifting toward the left and moving lower-brain activities into higher-up awareness.

It's reasonable to say that by using words to label your emotions, you're activating your left hemisphere. *Left* is where the words of *Language* hang out, as you might remember. So this is one technique you can use to get things shifting from the more "raw" emotions in the right toward the linguistic left. This shift means less alarm-based emotional reactivity and increased positive mood. Better balance.

In addition, you'll need to start bringing the upper brain online more by perceiving and attending to your body sensations in the moment. Doing this helps you shift the incoming body info from a lower-brain, unconscious process into your higher, "noticing" brain—giving you more action on the top.

We'll get into how to make these essential shifts later (they'll even be rolled into one meditation practice for you), but first, let's find you some company in your exploratory journey toward better emotional regulation.

Ron Versus the Volcano

Ron was 38 when he came in for his first-ever psychotherapy appointment, saying he never thought he'd "end up here." He'd never been married and hadn't ever had a long-term relationship.

He said he needed anger-management training. This, he said, was because everyone around him kept complaining about his frequent foul moods. In the preceding six months, his last girlfriend had broken up with him because she said she'd had enough of his "stewing volcano act"; his buddies were tired of how long he held grudges; and his boss had told him that he needed to "chill out, and fast," because his job was on the line.

Ron struggled mightily with intense, long-lasting anger. Something would happen (a disagreement, a friend canceling plans to get together, a disappointing performance review at work, someone cutting him off in traffic) and then his anger would precede him into every room for the rest of the day (or longer), and in a really big way. It was taking a toll on his body, too—he said that he caught every cold going around, couldn't ever sleep well, and often had headaches. His lack of emotional resilience was costing him a ton.

Pretty soon after meeting him, it became clear that Ron's vocabulary for his emotional experience was mostly either a pretty unconvincing "I'm okay" or "F*@# this."

He needed to wire in a dimmer switch so that he could grow away from being *too reactive, too quickly,* for *too long,* and *too biased* in one direction (anger) and toward being able to *quickly, nimbly,* and *more accurately* recognize and regulate his reactivity. He was a big football fan, so we talked about how he needed to shift away from his right hemisphere, the 300-pound linebacker, and get his left prefrontal cortex, the quarterback, in the game more often.

Ron and I talked about his history (and he also got a thorough medical checkup, which came back clean). He had the sense that everyone and everything depended on him to make things work. He'd felt that way since childhood, as early as he could recall, having had a mother with a progressive neurological disorder that left her needing more and more physical care. He'd loved his mother, and he'd sworn to himself when he was seven years old that she would never see him unhappy or upset about his ever-increasing role in helping her.

His mom had died a few years before our first meeting, and while Ron could acknowledge his anger about losing his mom (mostly raging at the doctors), he denied having felt any relief at the burden that was lifted, any sadness about the many years of sacrifices he'd made, any worry he might have had as a kid, or anything—just anger. Or a flat "I'm okay."

Ron recalled that that was the household's day-in-and-day-out response when he was growing up: a flat "I'm okay" or "We're okay." And—most confusing of all—"You're okay. No need to be upset." His mother had often said that to him as a way to try to soothe him (and, most likely, herself).

It was the kind of "regulation" of experiencing or expressing emotions that's really more like "restriction." Ron's mom, in her loving attempts to keep everything as low-key as possible, seemed to have had a hard time tuning in to her son's internal emotional state. In the absence of that attunement, Ron's brain had missed out on learning about noticing, labeling, and connecting to his emotions. All he had were breakthrough blasts of long-lasting anger that erupted in other places.

His brain had settled on the safest course it could find: sitting on a volcano of emotion, trying to stay numb. And so for years, since early childhood, his brain had been laying down wide, multilane neural highways to that suppressed-emotion volcano. For Ron, all of this added up to a volcanic "personality"—he would seem subdued and okay for long stretches, then suddenly anger would explode from him and stick to everything and everyone in sight.

Anger—and disconnection from all his other emotions—was serving Ron as a sort of safety zone. As long as he was braced and ready to protect himself by getting mad, he felt like he knew how the world worked, and in an odd way, he found that comforting.

Ron had a hard time even tolerating any conversation we might have about other feelings. He would get irritable (which he could recognize if I asked about it) and often physically reactive as well, getting antsy in his seat, picking intensely at the chair's armrest, or looking toward the door (which he was unaware of and tried to dismiss or deny if I mentioned it). He said that all he really wanted was a way to "stop blowing my top."

I told Ron about what was probably happening in his brain when the light switch went from "off" to 10,000 watts of "ON."

We talked about rewiring his brain to give it a variable voltage control—a dimmer switch—with a fully flexible range of settings.

And I told him that if he was interested, he'd need to practice the exercises I gave him once a day, starting with a five-minute dose, like taking medicine. "I know all about medicating on a regular schedule," he said. "I did it for my mother for 30 years."

Left-Right Balance and Emotional Resilience

You'll probably remember from Chapter 2 that having good communication and integration between your logical, linear, language-y left hemisphere and your nonverbal, "whole-picture," raw, spontaneous-emotion, stress-modulating right hemisphere is one of the major things we're working on with the meditation practices in this book. In Chapter 2, the focus was simply on integrating your two hemispheres so you could react authentically without shooting first and asking questions later. But integration isn't the only part of this equation; balance is also necessary, and that's the challenge we're going to tackle now.

Imagine yourself in a rowboat. Let's say you have one big, strong, muscular arm, and one that's puny and atrophied. As you row, you're likely to be moving in circles. Both arms are integrated in their movements—but one arm is going to dominate the direction in which you're traveling.

So, let's look a little more closely at creating greater *balance* between your right and left hemispheres. (Of course, just as with integration, whenever we're looking at any kind of balancing in your brain, it isn't just happening along one plane or between two parts. Whenever you do any of this, you're getting multiple layers of beneficial results.)

Some who study neuroscience look at the right side of the brain as key in responding to distress and uncomfortable emotions, with the overall strategy of "Get me outta here!" (also known as withdrawal behaviors).

The left side, in contrast, has been supported in some research as responding to positive, "nice" emotional states, with an attitude more like "Hey, let's move closer and get that good stuff!" (a.k.a. approach behaviors).

And guess what? There is a left-shift—that is, a shift in the balance of your brain's activity, in the direction of the left hemisphere—in people who practice mindfulness meditation. Not total left-brain dominance—just greater involvement of the left, making it easier to stay present, rather than retreating.

Too *much* left-brain activity and you're dominated by thoughts and mind-chatter, competing with the right brain's attendance to what's going on in the body and what raw emotions are percolating. You end up oblivious to much of anything else that's going on inside you or even the fullness of the real-life experience going on around you.

If your right brain is in charge, your roiling ocean of emotion is constantly sending crashing waves of unrelenting, unmodulated raw experience. So you're full of unprocessed, out-of-any-context stimulated responses.

Now, if your left brain and right brain are working as a balanced team, each bringing their own strengths . . . *yeah.* You can do your thinking *and* it'll be informed by what your body's reacting to and what your emotional brew is cooking up, without rowing in familiar circles.

So it's a "no-brainer" (oof) to say that left-right balance gives you a greater ability to notice and recognize your emotions, leading to fewer overly strong, overly long reactions. And you'll be making choices that aren't just *Piss off!* or *I'm outta here!*

"And How Does That Feel?"

The tired old cliché of what a psychotherapist always asks is, "And how did that make you feel?" Ugh.

As it turns out, though, putting your feelings into words seems to help integrate your brain—which helps regulate your emotions and perhaps even fends off depression. Show somebody a picture of an intense emotion (for example, a photo of a terrified-looking face), and activity in the amygdala spikes. Recent studies have shown that if you, looking at that same picture, were to verbally label the emotion, your amygdala's response would calm down, compared to what would happen if you simply observed it without labeling it.

It seems that the prefrontal cortex gets activated by the demand to come up with the word for the emotion. This leads a portion of the OMPFC to deliver some GABA to the amygdala, and GABA inhibits the amygdala's firing, basically telling it to shut up—so you're no longer in that primitive reactive state. Your parasympathetic brakes can slow you down, and your smart vagus gets you into social connection gear. This is a two-for-the-price-of-one deal: you're getting top-down *and* left-right integration/balance through the simple act of coming up with a word to describe your feeling.

There are many of us who are just not fluent in "feeling-type" words, so here's the first step: developing a basic vocabulary of words for feelings. For our purposes, what I've found to be most useful as a starting point is to get these "feeling categories" down:

- Mad
- Bad (as in ashamed)
- Sad
- Glad
- Scared

Call them "feeling-type" words, or "adjectives of emotions," or "affective labels" . . . whatever. Just start calling them.

Try it, right now. Come up with two or three feeling-type words for how you're feeling in this moment, while you're holding this book and you're being asked to bring your awareness and labels to your feelings. (Personally, for example, when a book "tells" me to do something, I sometimes get irritated.)

Pay attention to the sneaky ways you might try to veer off the feeling path and onto thoughts, evaluations, explanations, and so on. For example, a favorite I see in couples is "I feel that you're wrong." (That's a thought, and an evaluation of the other person.)

Another example of getting off track is "I feel misunderstood"—as in, "You are misunderstanding me." But how do you feel when you are misunderstood? Probably something along the lines of *sad* or *mad* or both.

Once people get the hang of labeling within these basic categories (mad-bad-sad-glad-scared), I encourage them to get a little more precise, perhaps using "I feel anxious" or "I'm feeling afraid" as more descriptive words for "scared." (If you need to expand your "feeling-type" vocabulary, as many people do, you might take a look at a website that lists over 4,000 of these words: *eqi.org/fw.htm.*)

It's important to note, as we're talking about *affective labeling* (using those feeling-type words to label your emotions), that there's a big difference between simply labeling a feeling—*describing* it—and *explaining* it, whether to yourself or to others. "Explanation" seems to engage a whole host of other activities, including judgments, interpretations, and defensiveness—which are influenced and potentially distorted by fear, your history, and so on.

So, keep it simple: just two or three single feeling-type words, and no "because."

Here's an example—Gail, married to Josh, would "shut down" (Josh's description, with which Gail agreed) whenever there was a disagreement between them, or even the potential for one. Her heart would pound, and the pit of her stomach would knot up, but all Josh could see was what he called Gail's "Easter Island" face. I gave Gail the following assignment: Whenever there was a disagreement brewing, she was to simply notice and label the feeling she was experiencing right then and there (or as soon as she was able). As soon as she was aware of anxiety stirring, she was to just plain say it out loud ("I'm feeling anxious")—period.

It was important that Gail really stop at just *labeling,* not describing or explaining it to herself or Josh. In the heat of the moment, we're really pretty rotten at describing the subtleties of emotion, and worse still at being able to accurately explain them. It also leads quickly down the paths of judging and defending—again, counterproductive.

Both Gail and Josh were surprised (*glad!*) that whenever Gail did this, she was able to unhook from her anxiety and the usual shut-down, take a break, get more grounded, and return to Josh in a much more productive, relationship-steadying state. Eventually Gail got better at doing it on the fly, and she didn't have to do it aloud—the mental notation was enough. It wasn't just a matter of Gail communicating her feelings to Josh. Rather, it was Gail's ability to be emotionally resilient—present and alive, without getting emotionally hijacked—that allowed their relationship much more room to grow and blossom.

I'd like to add here that many approaches to couples' therapy involve "improved communication skills," including saying what you're feeling. This is a great and helpful idea only if it's done in the context of helping both partners be better able to actually know what it is they're feeling! Even the best communication tools in the world won't help if you're essentially picking them randomly out of a bag and tossing them to your partner. Your capacity to be tuned in—body, brain, and mind—needs to be big and nimble, which won't be the case if you didn't get it while you were young, or if you haven't, as an adult, developed the ability to listen and respond in a more attuned way, without losing yourself in the process. That's where I've found most couples get stuck, and that's why I'm so committed to helping people develop these abilities.

By practicing mindfulness, becoming more aware of your emotional experience in the moment, and being able to consciously label it, you'll be integrating your brain to have less emotional reactivity and greater emotional resilience.

All Together Now

Ron, who, as you'll remember, had been struggling mightily to try to stop his angry outbursts, practiced his mindfulness exercises diligently and dutifully. He didn't like them at first, and for a while he kept reporting that the only feeling coming up during his meditation was "annoyance at having to do it." Occasionally he'd ask me to remind him of the details about how he was wiring up his dimmer switch, but he still wasn't sure he bought it.

After several weeks, he said that on some days, he'd think he'd been practicing the meditation for only 5 minutes, and it would actually have been closer to 20. He reported sleeping better and having fewer headaches. When he did feel a headache coming on, he was aware of it in enough time to drink some water and remember that the headaches weren't a "punishment" from his body. Instead, he started to view them as an "early warning system" indicating that he needed to ease up on himself.

He started to fidget less in our sessions when the subject of emotions came up. One day he spontaneously let me know that he usually felt "kind of uptight" on the mornings before our appointments. He surprised himself when he realized that he could describe where he'd felt that uptight-ness in his body (in his throat and jaw).

After about four months of regular practice, Ron's boss was so impressed by Ron's "levelheadedness" that he promoted him to a management position. His buddies were no longer avoiding him, and he'd noticed that he hadn't "blown his top" in a couple of months, except for one time in traffic—and even then, after a few minutes, he actually laughed at himself for how artfully he'd used an impressive string of profanities, and the bad mood was gone. He also wasn't getting sick as often.

Being with Ron had an entirely different feeling than it had when we'd started—he was much more at ease, and he had a much richer way of interacting—his responses were less clipped and had more descriptive language, but more important, he was able to meet me more in the middle in a way that felt more mutually collaborative and contingent. He seemed to actually inhabit his body, where he'd previously looked like he wanted to escape it. He'd also easily lost some weight that he'd struggled with, and he had started dating again. He said he felt as if he was finally getting the pieces of his life to come together—and he playfully rolled his eyes when I suggested that maybe it was because he'd gotten the pieces of his brain to come together.

Both sides of your brain are sitting there, waiting for you to wire them up and balance them out.

Ready?

"CAN YOU FEEL ME NOW?" MEDITATION

This meditation is intended to support left-right brain integration by tapping into the practice of labeling emotions with words—getting your left, linguistic, linear, logical hemisphere to work more routinely with your right, raw, body-information, spontaneous-reaction hemisphere. You're going to get more bang-for-buck than that, though, because at the same time, it supports vertical, bottom-to-top integration as well—developing the bridge between your deeper-down, "information directly from the body" limbic structures and your higher-up, "making sense of the experience I'm having" prefrontal cortex.

Begin by settling into your body. As in the Basic Mindfulness Meditation, gently and slowly lengthen your neck and spine by inviting your head to float upward a bit or by imagining a piece of string attached to the crown of your head pulling gently up. When you're ready, slowly close your eyes.

Take some easy time for a simple tour of your body to locate some sensation going on right now—the sensation of your breath passing through your nostrils; an itch; the pressure on your skin where your body meets the chair or where your feet meet the floor . . . physical sensations in the moment . . . your choice.

Your mind will quite naturally drift away from these sensations, toward other thoughts. The drifting and these thoughts are perfectly natural, and they aren't the enemy—you don't need to get rid of them. Your intention is simply to notice them when they happen and bring yourself back to the moment, to your current experience, so that the "story" of your thinking doesn't take you away. You're practicing awareness of the thoughts-and-words generation of your left hemisphere with the body-sensation detection of your right hemisphere.

When you notice thoughts arising, you might say to yourself, in a loving and friendly way, *Thinking . . . thinking.* Without criticizing or judging yourself or your thoughts (or criticizing yourself for criticizing yourself—one of my personal favorites!), return to the moment—return to the sensation you were focused on, or back to your breath, a great "safe harbor." To use a baseball analogy, your thoughts are like when you are running between bases. Your awareness of your breath in the moment is being on a base, safe and steady.

Emotions may come up too. Sometimes, as soon as you become aware of them, they pass; other times, they ask for more of your attention. While you may not be aware of it at first, with practice you'll begin to notice that along with an emotional reaction, there is an accompanying experience in your body.

For example, if you become aware of feeling anxious, you might notice that your gut is also a bit tight. The other side of that same helpful coin is that you might first notice that your gut feels tight and then become aware that you're feeling anxious. These are both opportunities to integrate your brain, top to bottom and bottom to top.

As emotions arise in your mind or your body, invite yourself to come up with a "feeling-type" word. In a gentle and friendly way, without trying to get rid of the emotion, let that label be spoken in your mind (for example, *Sadness . . . sadness*) as you invite yourself to compassionately investigate the "this moment" physical experience of the emotion: Where in your body do you feel it, in this moment? What might you notice about it—does it seem to have a texture? Edges? Weight? Is it static or dynamic? Does it change—does it move, increase, diminish—as you maintain your awareness of it?

Continue to sit, moving between noticing, labeling, and experiencing.

Sometimes you'll find that there don't seem to be any emotions coming up. In response to that, you might have some thoughts, like *Is this normal?* or *Am I doing this right?* When you become aware of thoughts like these, see if there might be a thread connecting them to something going on in your body—maybe a furrowing of your brow? A change in your breathing?

Often, as emotions come up, your mind will (again, quite naturally) drift—or maybe leap!—into thoughts, analysis, or judgment about the emotion. When this happens, gently and lovingly bring yourself back to the moment, back to base, back to your breath. Know that the stronger the emotion, the more you'll "want" to have thoughts about it (or thoughts that take you away from it) and to leave your in-the-moment experience of it.

With the consideration and gentleness with which you'd say it to a dear friend, remind yourself that you are simply having the experience of an emotion—you don't need to react to it, understand it, or analyze it in this moment. Your only task right now is to experience the emotion, use a word to label it, and invite yourself to gently investigate where you might be feeling it in your body. Understanding your emotions is a task for another time.

You'll find yourself moving back and forth between experiencing, thinking-and-returning, and sensing in your body, probably in some pretty repetitive loops—which are exquisitely perfect for your purpose! The more opportunities you get for becoming aware of "detaching" into thinking and then choosing to return to the breath, the emotion, and the body sensation of it, the more you are building integrated neural connections (*top-down/bottom-up* and *right-left/left-right*) for emotional resilience.

When you're ready to end your meditation, take a few slow breaths, slightly deeper, still easy and unforced. With your eyes still closed, bring your "mind's eye" to an image of the room you're sitting in, of what you'll see when you open your eyes. Then slowly open or refocus your eyes. Still sitting and breathing naturally, slowly take a look at the room around you, and gently reenter your day.

CHAPTER 6

Grounded Electrical Outlets

Response Flexibility

When I was a kid, our house was struck by lightning. Fortunately, we were away when it happened. The house didn't have a lightning rod to direct the powerful jolt of raw electricity safely down and out, so the surge, seeking ground, zipped along all of the fast-conducting metal it could find—vent pipes, plumbing, and wires.

As the electrical surge traveled, it ignited any combustible materials along the way—wood, insulation, plastic, you name it. It was simply following its prime directive, according to the laws of physics: get to ground. One response, inflexible and impressively destructive. Half the house burned down. Even the necessary actions to put the fire out were destructive: the entire contents of the attic and bedrooms had been flung out of the second story, and the place was drowned in water.

Now that you're heading off being hijacked by fear and gaining the ability to recover with emotional resilience, you're ready to improve your capacity to respond with greater flexibility—even in the heat of the moment of an emotionally charged situation—from a wider, more beneficial range of possibilities than lightning bolts and firefighters.*

Response Inflexibility: Dating Thunderbolts

Kind of like lightning when it hits ungrounded pipes and wiring, our histories of emotionally painful experiences can lead us to surge emotionally when we're reminded of them, whether implicitly or explicitly. And we often have a fairly limited repertoire of responses to those situations that just set us off—rage, tears, going silent, checking out. The surge and the reflexive fire-department response leave you vulnerable to making a real mess when you don't mean to.

One of my patients, Julia, came to see me because she kept dating men whom she couldn't trust to stick around. She'd "get a feeling" that they weren't going to be able to be in a relationship for the long run. She said she kept freaking out and abruptly ending relationships because at some point she'd just know that she couldn't trust the guy.

Julia had an aliveness that was palpable, with a beautifully expressive face and a colorful, engaging way of talking. As we talked about her early relationship history, she said she had great parents and felt very close to both of them, even though they'd divorced when she was very young and had lived on opposite coasts while she was growing up. She'd lived with her mother and traveled by plane to visit her father fairly often. Her father, she said, was always loving and clear during these reunions and separations; he would always tell her that she didn't need to worry, because he was always there for her and would never leave her. "See? He's a really

* I am in fact deeply grateful to firefighters and their bold actions. It's just that the approach doesn't work so well when it comes to intimate relationships.

great guy. With a father like that, why am I so screwed up when it comes to men?"

During the course of our work together, Julia dated a few different men, and I got to hear in (nearly) real time about several of her freak-outs. Eventually, she got to the point where she was more conscious of the men she was choosing, and she got better at selecting guys who were less likely to provoke "early freaking." But she still had these slash-and-burn responses to even the slightest whiff of potential abandonment.

At one point, Greg, a man whom she was dating quite seriously, said, "I know you can get freaked out with guys, but really, I'll always be here for you. I'm not going to leave you." Julia told me, "I immediately freaked out, and we got into a huge fight. What the hell is wrong with me?"

I shared how struck I was that Greg's words were the same soothing message that her father had offered her over and over in her childhood—and suddenly tears of grief and pain all but exploded from Julia's eyes. After her sobs subsided, she realized that in her earliest attachment experience to a man (her dad), the reassurance—"I'll always be here for you"—went along with the reality of being left. Little Julia had had to manage her loss, reunion, and loss again in each visit and separation with her dad, whom she adored. He was in many ways an amazing father, and her experience was that he did always love her warmly and dearly, with the very best of intentions. But the unintentional pain and confusion had made an early and stubborn impression on her brain's wiring, and those long-ago wired pathways caught fire like a house struck by lightning whenever those old triggers arced into her brain.

What are the surges in the brain that are behind those habits—the ones that cause us to respond so reactively, reflexively, and rigidly? What can you do to have a greater range of response choices available than just that old-wired habit of *get to ground?*

"Hark, the Cannon Roars!"

It'll be helpful to get clear about what we're aiming for here: response flexibility. It's all about choice.

And being able to make good, relationship-enhancing choices, instead of knee-jerk reactions, means that you need to have a moment—seriously, milliseconds—to give yourself a chance to make a choice. The lightning that struck my house? It only had one choice. By cultivating mindfulness, you give your brain the ability to choose to respond mindfully.

We all have those *d'oh* moments when we realize we've blown it with our partners and said something we regretted. And we've all had the experience where, upon later reflection (sometimes days later), we finally let the authentic, meaningful response that we *wish* we'd had the presence of mind to come out with earlier bubble up into our awareness.

By practicing mindfulness meditation, you'll give your brain more time to generate an awareness of choices. The skills and wiring you've been learning as you've been reading and practicing your meditation exercises are enabling you to:

1. Prevent your body and your primitive fear from driving you into a reflexive emotional ditch (or worse)—which Chapters 3 and 4 helped you get started on;
2. Consciously assess the incoming information and recover with resilience from emotional misfiring (as you've discovered in Chapters 4 and 5); and
3. Give your higher brain the chance it needs to kick it up a notch and choose from a broader, healthier array of potential responses—the subject of this chapter.

Far easier said than done, for most of us. How on earth, in the heat of the moment, with lightning racing through your brain, do you manage to *pause?* It reminds me of a venerable old joke:

> A struggling actor finally gets a speaking part. He has one line: "Hark, the cannon roars." The director tells him it's

so simple, he doesn't need to come to rehearsals—just memorize the line and show up on opening night.

He tries it out a thousand ways: "Hark, the cannon roars." Practices it at work: "Hark, the cannon roars." At night: "Hark, the cannon roars." On the bus, very softly: "Hark, the cannon roars." Opening night, backstage, he's dressed, he's ready, waiting in the wings for his cue, and he rehearses one more time, under his breath: "Hark, the cannon roars."

Finally, his cue comes up. He walks onstage, and suddenly the stage-prop cannon issues an earthshaking BOOM! He flings himself to the ground and screams, "What the f*@# was that?!"

Even the most insightful and intellectually capable people lose it when the cannon roars and their amygdala gets hijacked (a phrase used by Daniel Goleman, PhD,[1] that I love). How can you get the rest of your brain—the higher-level, insightful, rational parts that Goleman, Daniel Siegel, and others refer to as "the high road"—to jump on board and prevent that lightning bolt from blowing things to smithereens?

Help from Above

The higher centers of your brain—from the upper areas of your limbic system and on up a bit to your prefrontal cortex—are your buddies who, together, afford you the ability to generate more response choices, to respond to your partner more flexibly. In case you've forgotten your well-placed friends, they include the following linked-up, geographically clustered structures:

- Just behind your forehead, mostly in the middle, you've got your OMPFC, which seems to be related to your ability to put the brakes on before you respond, including calming, relational, and flexibility functions.

- You've got your anterior cingulate cortex (ACC), which does a lot of cool stuff, but for our purposes, its two important functions are related to paying attention and putting together thoughts and feelings.
- And last but definitely not least, there's your insula, helping to integrate and run info back and forth between the prefrontal cortex, the limbic system, and the body. Having these converging streams seems to let us put incoming information into context. (And how many times have you screwed up because you didn't consider things in context?)

(Brief reminder about the "cheat" in Chapter 2—all of these brain parts can be shorthanded as your *basal forebrain*.)

When all these are tuned up, well linked, and fully online, you've got your body, your emotions, your thinking, your awareness in the moment, and your sense of self all ready to help you *pause and choose your response* when, say, your well-intentioned husband clogs up the kitchen sink . . . and you're in the middle of preparing dinner for 20 . . . including your food-snob mother-in-law.

You get to be more than just a Pavlovian dog that starts salivating at every bell just because that's the response that's been trained up. Your middle prefrontal structures help you to engage in flexible, right-for-the-moment responses.

Hitting the Pause Button

To be able to reduce your hair-trigger, "not-thought" body reactivity, you need the areas of your brain which respond to the threat (most of your limbic brain) to have a fast and reliable conduit running back and forth to the more "reasonable" part of your brain, which is up a little higher. Ah, yes, your basal forebrain.

Having that "fast and reliable conduit"—in other words, having your lower, emotionally reactive limbic brain well linked to the basal forebrain—means that you can have a few more milliseconds to evaluate what you initially sensed as a potential danger.

A longer pathway buys you more time to consult with your wiser, more circumspect, and less hair-triggered prefrontal cortex. You have a chance to de-escalate the sounding of the alarm, get your smart vagus to calm things down in your body, and move in the direction of greater ease.

"But I Thought I Was Supposed to Keep It Real—?"

There's a myth that won't seem to die in the popular understanding of anger. Back in the 1960s, psychology (doing the best it could as a very young science) put forth the notion that "venting" your anger, letting it all hang out, was the way to go if you wanted to be emotionally healthy.

Venting (a.k.a. *cathartic expression of anger*) feels great in the moment, and it would seem to make sense that letting it out, instead of keeping it bottled up, would be a good idea, like letting some steam out of a cranked-up pressure-cooker.

Nope.

In the 1990s, research definitively showed that letting off steam actually leaves you more prone to do it again and again (it does feel good, after all). Venting keeps your nervous system primed for more angry responses, and you're more likely to *keep* venting and *stay* more primed for angry outbursts.

Whatever you practice the most is what gets wired up to be the first and fastest route in your brain. And the "hit" of dopamine that you probably get from venting makes it all the more addictive.

Not the path to better relationships.

"Yuh Cahn't Get Theah from Heeah"

With early experiences of optimal, attuned communication and secure attachment, our brains have more experience of "taking the high road" and therefore have more ready-for-action wiring in the middle prefrontal areas. Shunting the surge of reaction upward into the prefrontal centers (those middle prefrontal areas in particular) is, quite literally, second nature for those who grew up with brains that had those experiences.

But what about those of us who didn't get that?

Or who are able to keep it together and use our higher-brain processes in certain contexts (like, at work), but elsewhere (at home after a long day), not so much?

You may have tried various strategies and/or made lots of resolutions (*I'm not going to blow up at Bob when he forgets to ______*, or *Whenever I feel myself getting defensive, I'm going to take three deep breaths before I respond*).

Those strategies and thoughts can be helpful, but how many of us forget those well-intentioned promises to ourselves in the heat of the moment? (My hand is raised, how about yours?) To remember and choose to engage those strategies, you've got to be able to recruit, pretty much immediately, your higher brain. But your limbic brain is simply, naturally faster on the draw.

So how *do* we get there from here?

Carnegie Hall

> Guy gets lost in Manhattan.
>
> He asks a passerby, "Excuse me, how do I get to Carnegie Hall?"
>
> The passerby answers, "Practice, practice, practice."

You guessed it—practice mindfulness.

Mindfulness practice grows the connections from down low to up high and in between all of those helpful buddies in your basal forebrain, making those connections (and the structures themselves, it seems) thicker and speedier. Instead of reactivity reverberating and ricocheting around on its own, the more "insightful" parts of the brain get called in. And the more connections that get made between the lower and the upper parts of your brain, and between the left and the right hemispheres, the more emotional responses are possible.

As your middle prefrontal areas get better integrated, the pathways get longer and more complex, and that is the pause that refreshes.

Who's Got Time for All That?

Based on what we know about how fast various parts of the brain respond to input, you have your quick 50-millisecond initial response from your amygdala and then your "slow" 500-millisecond response from your higher cortex. That sounds like a *huge* difference, but let's think about it a little more. How long is 500 milliseconds? Choose whichever one gives you the best perspective:

- one-half of a second;
- an eighth note at one beat per second (metronome marking = 60);
- one-half of one healthy adult heartbeat; or
- slightly more than the blink of an eye (an eye blink = 300–400 milliseconds in humans).

So, all you need is a split second—literally—to prevent the lightning from burning down the house.

What you're aiming for is the 500 milliseconds it seems to take for the messages from the limbic areas to travel up through to the prefrontal areas, and for those areas to activate your awareness—so you can start generating the possibility of alternative responses.

The Road Less Traveled

Cultivating a practice of mindfulness gets the "lightning bolts" to activate not just your brain's low-road limbic responses, but also your high-road "thinking" processes. It's like installing a lightning rod that automatically trips the circuit breaker. Except instead of just turning off the power like a circuit breaker, it actually *gives* you the power to make better choices of how to respond.

Let's take a look back at Julia. Her intellectual understanding of the connection to her young experiences was helpful, but not adequate. After we talked about her brain's wiring dilemma and why it was short-circuiting her ability to stay in a relationship, she started regular mindfulness meditation. At other times throughout her day, she also practiced taking little "pauses."

Julia felt gradual and steady improvement, and within a couple of months she was able to see that her emotional responses to potential relationship losses were no longer of the "lock, load, and fire" variety, but that she could actually make conscious, "in-the-moment," mindful choices about how to respond. She seemed most surprised that it didn't feel like she was just cramming her real responses down, but honoring what was true and saying it more clearly than she ever had before. She was able to slow herself down enough to make good relationship choices instead of freaking out.

One year after they'd started dating, Julia exuberantly accepted Greg's proposal of marriage.

A Pause to Refresh You

Before we get to the meditation practice in this chapter, I'd like to offer you a quick six-second exercise that you can do at any time of day to supplement the overall grounding benefits you'll get from formal meditation. (Practicing anything, even for six seconds, can help rewire your brain.)

When I was ten years old—and suffering from anxious insomnia—my father taught me this simple way to slow down the breakneck pace that sometimes gripped me and/or to break the autopilot trance I so often fell into. I could pull this little exercise out whenever I needed it, and I've been doing so for years. By using this exercise, you'll be creating a habit in your brain of taking a pause. You can help your brain be more automatic in being less automatic—meaning that you can make it easier for your brain to have the lightning-fast, automatic response of pausing instead of emotionally knee-jerking it every time.

As Tara Brach, PhD (a meditation teacher, psychologist, and founder of the Insight Meditation Community of Washington, D.C.), wrote, "a pause is a suspension of activity, a time of temporary disengagement when we are no longer moving toward any goal . . . [when] we stop asking, 'What do I do next?'" She goes on, "[When] we resume our activities . . . we do so with increased presence and more ability to make choices."[2]

It can be 1 second, 6 seconds, or 60 seconds. I personally like the six-second pause, partly because that's how I learned it from my father (who used it to great effect as part of his work as a psychologist with veterans), and because I can usually find a measly six seconds at least a few times a day. Here's what it might look like:

- Choose your cue. It might be something "external," like your phone ringing, or more "internal," like noticing that you're suddenly jiggling your foot or wearing your shoulders as earrings.
- Say a simple, kind phrase to yourself, like *Alert mind, calm body.*
- Inhale an easy breath through your nose, imagining the breath coming up from the bottoms of your feet and flowing through your body (your ankles, calves, thighs, hips, torso, neck, shoulders, arms, and hands). Invite the feeling of flowing warmth and pleasant heaviness to enter and settle in.
- As you exhale, let your jaw, tongue, and shoulders go loose, with a wave of pleasant heaviness and warmth flowing down your body, carrying away the tension from your face, neck, shoulders, arms, chest, back, stomach, hips, legs, ankles, and out the bottom of your feet. Then slowly resume your normal activity.

I don't recommend starting to learn a "pause practice" in the middle of heated interactions with others—that would be like trying to change a fuse when the lamp is already on fire. Rather, practice pausing at other, less loaded times; you'll be installing a better lightning rod for the relationship bolts, so it'll be there to handle the surge when you need it. When you consciously make a habit of pausing, it becomes something your brain and body do without your having to think about it.

You can create the habit of pausing throughout the day in a variety of ways. Experiment to see which work best for you:

- At the beginning of every hour, no matter what you're doing
- Whenever you get into your car, before you turn the key
- Just before eating
- Before responding to an e-mail, sending a tweet, or posting on Facebook
- Any time you turn on a faucet—taking a shower, washing your hands, doing the dishes, getting a drink of water

Okay, you've got that little gem in your back pocket now. It'll come in handy, making you notice, farther in advance, when the electrical surges, emotional urges, or "waves" are coming—six seconds to notice the wave starting to swell gives you some time to grab your surfboard. Being more mindful doesn't mean not having your feelings, your thoughts, or your urges to react—it means being more aware of what's going on and making more mindful choices.

"CATCH A WAVE" MEDITATION

Julia found the meditation exercise below, inspired by addiction-treatment pioneer Alan Marlatt, PhD, to be helpful in being more in charge of her urges to emotionally explode in the face of intense feelings. If she noticed an urge toward her habit of "freaking out," she could "surf" the urges—noticing that, like waves, they'd swell and subside if she stayed with them.

Since this meditation does invite you to stay with feelings that you may have been avoiding for a long time, remember to be gentle with yourself, and seek support and guidance if you need it.

As in the Basic Mindfulness Meditation Instructions, settle into your body and your breath.

Bringing your awareness to your body, you'll probably notice some sensation, some discomfort such as an itch, a sore muscle, a feeling of restlessness, or a desire to shift your position.

Settle your awareness on one of those sensations or desires, one of those *urges*, and see what thoughts come up.

If I don't scratch this itch, I'm gonna go crazy . . . I have to scratch, really . . . I'm not gonna scratch, I'll just notice the itch (in a calm inner voice) . . . I'm not gonna scratch, I'm just supposed to notice the itch (in a cranky inner voice) . . . What if it's a bug? . . . Oh, man, I want to scraaaatch . . .

All your thoughts are just thoughts, just momentary neuro-events—they're not who you are. They don't *have* to be acted on. You can just notice them. And as in other meditation sessions, you'll probably notice your mind going to other thoughts, too—*How long have I been sitting here? . . . This is never gonna work for me; I'm the world's worst meditator . . . Did Danny remember his lunch this morning?*

Those are also just thoughts. For now, just notice that your mind has wandered and, with gentle kindness, bring yourself back to the sensation or urge you were focusing on.

We often have an urge to control our discomforts, be they itches or thoughts or feelings we don't like. Rather than feeling them and being aware of them, we mindlessly rush to make them better—to fix them (as is often the case for people who have a anxious pattern of attachment and/or a noisy right hemisphere that tends to drive their emotions)—or to detach from them, ignore them, or do whatever it takes to try to flee from what we think their source is (as Julia tended to do, with her pattern of attachment and highly right-hemisphere-dominant, raw-emotion way of living).

You don't have to be "wiped out" or "rolled under" by the waves. Rather, breathe and maintain a gentle balance, feeling when you start to lean too hard in one direction or another. Allow the wave to support you as you ride each swell and trough.

One of the things that Julia noticed, and that I and many others have, too, is that as you surf your urges and notice your thoughts, whenever you come back to the sensation or urge that was the initial focus, it's changed.

By practicing this kind of "urge surfing," you're building your capacity to bring a more integrated brain to bear on your experiences. You're improving your ability to bring your focused attention to them. In that way, you're able to have this experience in explicit memory, where you can deal with it consciously, instead of shoving it, too, into the attic of implicit memories that drive us without our awareness.

CHAPTER 7

Putting a Work Light in the Attic

Insight/Self-Knowing

Now that you've explored the preceding chapters, you're on your way to developing a much broader, more stable base when it comes to your emotions. That equipment will help you tremendously in our next exploration—going into your internal "attic" (your attachment and relationship history). Understanding more about "how did I get here?" and "why do I respond like that to closeness?" gives you an even greater capacity to build healthier relationships in your here and now. In essence, you've created a safe harbor, so we can now go into deeper exploration of what makes you tick.

Take a look at Thomas, who walked into my office dressed impeccably in a suit and tie and somehow, despite the 95-degree humid summer heat outside, unwrinkled and cool. He sat carefully in the chair across from me, briefly assessing the room. With a chuckle, he said, "So this is where you're going to tell me what's wrong with me, huh?"

Thomas had so much going for him on the outside. He was stunningly handsome, and he had multiple degrees from the finest schools, an amazing job, and by his report, a luxurious, beautifully decorated home. At times, I felt as though I were sitting with an exquisitely crafted Fabergé egg. But for all of his 40 years Thomas had kept himself from believing that there was anything inside worth looking at.

Not that he thought of himself as worthless inside (at least, not consciously—more about that in a bit). He was simply certain that looking inside one's self was pointless. "Why do I have to dig around inside? Just tell me what I need to do to make my marriage better."

At one point in an early session, he took out a notebook and poised his pen, asking me to dictate what he should say to his wife to appease her. All he needed was some advice.

He sincerely believed that none of his experiences or relationships as a kid growing up had anything to do with who he was now. He did acknowledge that having parents who encouraged him to excel in school, which resulted in his being accepted by all his top choices for colleges (and then top grad schools), had had a "salutary effect."

Thomas would get perplexed when I'd ask him to tell me about his childhood relationships with his brothers and sisters, his parents, friends, teachers—anyone.

"Really, I'm not hiding anything. I just don't remember much about stuff like that. I mean, I know I had a good childhood. It's not like I'm blanking stuff out—I remember the names of my old teachers, when my family's birthdays are, all kinds of stuff. I can tell you exactly what our house looked like—heck, I can even tell you what kind of dog food we gave the dog."

When I asked about times he might remember getting upset emotionally when he was little, and what he would do, Thomas replied, "Hmm . . . I remember when I broke my leg playing soccer, if that's what you mean. It hurt, but it's not like I got all upset or anything. I got a cast, it healed."

How did his parents respond when he broke his leg? "It was no big deal, really. I mean, they took me to the doctor, and I remember my mother cut my pants to fit over the cast. It's pretty normal for a five-year-old kid to break something, right?"

I noticed that Thomas's voice was a little tighter now, and that his breath was a bit more shallow.

Did he remember being held by either of his parents when he got hurt or sick? "Y'know, I don't remember. I'm sure they did whatever they were supposed to do. But it's not like I remember every hug or anything."

Any physical affection? "I just don't remember much from back then."

Flash forward to the present: Thomas's main reason for coming in to see me was because his wife of two years was complaining that "she can't tell whether or not I love her" and that he was not helping her enough with their infant son, and "because she just can't let go of the fact that I had a couple of meaningless one-night stands" during their engagement.

He went on: "She says I need to figure out why I did it. I think I just need to make sure I don't do it again. We have a perfectly fine marriage—we've never had a fight, we both like to do the same things, we have a great house, a healthy kid, it's fine. It's a little boring, but that's normal married life."

Getting to Know . . . *You*

Ever been in an attic where everything's just been kind of shoved up there—no labels, no dates, no organization? Now add a low, sloped roof, with overhead rafters you can't see. Oh, and one of those attic floors where only part of it has floorboards—the rest is just insulation, lying on the top of the ceiling below.

And no light.

That cluttered attic and its contents are, as you might have guessed, a metaphor for aspects of your brain and your experiences. It's a quietly busy place that's constantly informing you about who you are, how the world works, and what it means to be in a relationship.

How did I get here? Why do I keep feeling/thinking/responding /behaving this way? Getting to know and understand yourself in a real way, looking beyond the surface level of your actions and your thoughts—and having a *coherent narrative framework* for how you got to be you—gives you an internal attic "work light." You get to understand what the buried thoughts and stories are that silently guide you (and sometimes shove you around) in how you think of your "self" and others.

You're then far less vulnerable to getting lost in the dark, tripping over dusty boxes—or even falling through the ceiling—when it comes to being in relationship with others.

Memories and the Corners of Your Mind

Remember that experiences cause your neurons to fire, and that neurons that fire together, wire together. In this way, the experiences you have shape your brain.

Also remember that we all have *implicit memories,* some of which formed when you were very young, before much of your brain was really online. These memories got quickly and permanently stored, even though you don't have conscious awareness of them as memories—they're just kind of "in there," informing and influencing you *without any kind of time stamp, and without your being aware of their influence.* We talked about this before as the "unthought known."

Another way to think of your implicit memories is that they are *unconscious effects of your past experiences.* Here are some important things to consider about these implicit, "timeless" memories. Take your time reading these points—they're simple on the surface, but carry some pretty big implications.

- Implicit memories are nonverbal "recordings" of experiences that are related to emotion, behavior, perceptions, and (most likely) sensations in the body formed when the hippocampus isn't online to organize and contextualize experiences. If they had been contextualized by the hippocampus, they would be explicit memories—those memories that you remember on purpose.

- Implicit memory hangs out mostly in the right hemisphere of your brain. The right hemisphere, as a reminder, has heavy-duty connections to your lower-level limbic structures, as well as a strong influence on your "withdraw" or "avoid" decisions.
- All your memories from before you were about 18 months old are implicit memories, because your brain wasn't developed enough to do much else with them. Your hippocampus simply wasn't up to the task of explicit memory tagging. And most of the memories you were creating at that point in your life dealt with interacting with your primary caregivers. Your little life depended utterly upon them, after all. So your young brain put a very high premium on making sure you remembered and learned from those relationship experiences, what it meant to be "attached," storing those memories well and deep. Even though those early experiences are vital in your social and emotional learning and to your subsequent relationship behaviors, you have virtually no conscious memory of them.
- Even beyond those early years—up to age four or five—the large majority of your memories are implicit. Forming explicit memories (which we'll talk about more below) requires conscious, focused attention, via your hippocampus. You simply aren't able to pay attention in a focused way to the millions of experiences, sensations, and so on that you're constantly having. So, much of the time, that stuff just gets tucked away in implicit memory.

- In addition to those earliest times in your brain's development, and all those subsequent experiences that you weren't paying attention to, implicit memories are formed at other times when your hippocampus, for a variety of reasons, isn't online. Certain sleep medications, and alcohol, for example, can throw the hippocampus offline, so your experiences while using those may be stored as implicit memories. Research into extreme emotional states, such as rage and terror, is showing that when stress hormones (such as cortisol) flood the brain, the hippocampus is much less available.
- While implicit memories don't have words or other cognitive "tags" attached to them, they do have other ways of letting themselves be known. When an implicit memory gets called up by something in the here and now, you won't know it's a memory—you'll just experience it through emotions, behaviors, and (in all likelihood) body sensations as well, such as a tightening in your throat or the pressure of tears coming to your eyes. You'll feel it but won't know that it's an echo from the past. You'll probably attribute that anxious (or angry or excited) feeling that seems to come out of nowhere to whatever you're currently experiencing (like that date at the circus we discussed earlier). Not because you're dense—but because there's no tag or time stamp on it to tell you that the feeling is an implicit memory from the attic.

Like the boxes and rafters and unsupported floors in the attic that we can't see well, our implicit memories are the stuff that often trips us up. We can't measure implicit memory directly, we can't directly retrieve it, we don't even know when it's in play—and yet it has a tremendous influence on how we respond to the world, how we "are" in relationships, even our self-concept *(Am I lovable?)* and self-regulation *(What do I do about feeling hurt?)*.

The bottom line is that our attachment styles are implicit memories, "unthought knowns" that shape our relationships in amazingly powerful ways, yet mostly from in the shadows.

Now let's take a deeper look at *explicit memory.* That's the stuff that you consciously retrieve:

"Remember the vacation when Robbie kept tying my shoelaces together?"

"Oh, man, I've always hated the circus—I remember when my parents took me. I was four, and the clowns scared the daylights out of me."

"Wait, what's the name of my cousin's youngest kid? A, B, C, D, E . . . Earl! That's it."

- Explicit memory is the stuff that most people think of when they talk about memory (or forgetfulness)—long-term memory, short-term memory, and the very important episodic and autobiographical forms of memory.
- When an explicit memory comes up, you're aware that it's a memory—that it's a recollection of an experience you've had in the past that you're remembering while you're in the here and now.
- To store an explicit memory, you need a nice, big, working hippocampus—and *focused attention.* Okay, pay attention now: focused attention is a skill that we know improves when you practice mindfulness—and there are studies that show an increase in the volume of the hippocampus in people who practice mindfulness.

Your Thoughts Aren't You

We tend to want to believe our thoughts (and feelings and behaviors) are the root of who we are. As we've talked about, though, your thoughts (and feelings and behaviors) are neurological events that happen in milliseconds. Another millisecond later, another thought (feeling, behavior) comes along.

You know that the fleeting neurological events you've had so far have wired and shaped your brain; the way your brain is wired and shaped then shapes your subsequent thoughts, feelings, and behaviors.

And you know that your thoughts are shaped and prodded and informed in significant ways by your implicit memories, often without your awareness.

So, if you can shed some light on that attic stuff, those packed-away clues and souvenirs of how you came to be you, you can potentially change how you think, your emotional stance, your behavioral habits, the choices you make, and how your relationships with yourself and others go.

As Daniel Siegel, MD, says, "If you can make sense of your story, you can change it."[1]

It boils down to this: Your thoughts are not who you are. Your thoughts are basically momentary neurological events that shape your brain. Provoke different thoughts—different neurological events—and you provoke a different "you."

Attachment ←→ Well-Being ←→ Coherent Narrative

Researchers on attachment have listened closely to the ways in which adults respond to questions about their childhood experiences and relationships. They listen for a *coherent narrative* when adults tell them about their lives. They're not just being nosy; having a sense of who you are and how you came to be this way—and being able to articulate your history in a way that hangs together —turns out to be an important predictor of your own capacity for healthy, secure attachment.

Once you listen to the narrative of your life and pay attention to where the blocks might be and where the blanks might be, you have much more powerful self-knowledge and insight—a work light in the attic—affording you greater awareness of where to focus to improve your relationships. Coherent narratives and brain integration go hand in hand. You need the cortical, higher-up levels of the brain to be integrated with the lower-down, subcortical, limbic levels. You need the left hemisphere and the right to be integrated. Within and between, side to side and up and down, your brain needs to have its structures and their functions working together to come up with your story of "You."

So having a coherent narrative means getting all those brain parts working together in an integrated way. Or maybe it goes in the other direction: getting all those brain parts working together in an integrated way means you gain the capacity for a coherent narrative . . .?

What we do know from attachment research is that a coherent narrative is related to emotional well-being. We also know that having an integrated brain is connected to emotional well-being. Which is the chicken and which is the egg?

It seems that it could go in both directions. Growing up in an environment that supports secure attachment promotes emotional well-being, as well as a coherent narrative. Your brain, in forming the coherent narrative, is integrating in many different directions and between many different structures—it's installing a well-integrated wiring system. And, flowing back in the other direction, your well-being, from the secure attachment, affords you the ability to form a coherent narrative.

And if you didn't grow up in that way? Looking inside yourself and developing a coherent narrative as an adult seems to help support the same kind of emotional well-being, and, it would appear, the same kind of integrated brain wiring, that you might have missed out on as a kid.

For many years, I couldn't tell certain stories from my childhood without the old emotions I'd experienced back then flooding me (and flooding many tissues with tears and snot). Those issues were so unresolved for me that my brain "dis-integrated" a bit whenever I brought them up. And, because they weren't part of a coherent, integrated narrative, they leaked into how I lived my adult life as well, even when I didn't consciously bring them up.

Other people have a bare-bones tale of their childhood: "My parents were great. I don't remember them telling me they loved me, but I'm sure they did." Period. End of narrative. If, as you tell the story you have of your life, it's mostly "just the facts, ma'am," that's a pretty good clue about how well those brain areas involved in coherent narratives are (or aren't) working together—and about where you may be hitting a glass ceiling in your current relationship life as well.

As for Thomas, he was able to report facts of his childhood, but they were sparse and didn't hang together like a story. Even more important, his reporting didn't include anything about what it was like emotionally—how he felt when the family dog died, or when his dad came home from work, stone-faced and silent, only to hide behind the newspaper. His autobiographical memory contained little of the right-brain, feeling memory, because that part of his wiring had been neglected.

Maybe your narrative has few emotional components, little self-inclusion, or skips around in time: "My mother made sure she taught us right from wrong. The other day, one of my co-workers crossed in the middle of the street, but me? No way. I went to the crosswalk. My mother had rules, I'm sure—they're just so much a part of me I can't even remember them, but you can be damned sure there were rules."

When we're talking about looking at your narrative, it's not about whether or not your memory is factually accurate, but whether the story as you remember it has coherence—whether it hangs together, has emotional texture as well as factual pieces, and so on. It's not "The Truth" of your past that we're after—it's your experience of it.

Tuning in to your narrative is important because it can give you important information about your understanding of yourself. It provides you with clues about where the integration of your brain needs work and what your potential obstacles are when it comes to relationships. Listening to Thomas, for example, it was clear that his early experiences had led him to have a dismissive, avoidant stance when it came to relationships and emotions. His narrative was limited to "just the facts," without emotional colors, without even any sense of one fact being connected to another. That's sort of a bread-crumb trail of what his earliest, implicit memories around attachment might be. If his parents had been emotionally unavailable or distant (as it sounded while I listened to him), the very young Thomas probably figured out—in the interests of minimizing his emotional pain, and of surviving—that pulling away emotionally and avoiding any reliance on others was the best possible choice back then.

For young Thomas, it appeared that trying for more warmth and more connection was met most often with practical functionality from his parents, a cold shoulder—which, to the developing brain, is labeled as stressful, a bad thing to be avoided, the way a toddler who touches a hot stove or gets snapped at by a dog learns not to do *that* again.

Thomas learned to tune out information inside him—emotions, bodily sensations, or any of the ways in which we tune in to ourselves or others. During the time when his implicit memories of attachment were first forming, emotions and their ilk were nothing more than liabilities.

Thomas's reliance on his higher-cortical, logical, rational, unemotional, distant way of getting through the world served him exceptionally well when he was little. It continued to give him some pretty good benefits as he went through all those years of school, and it worked for him in his current job, too. He really was doing the best he knew how.

You've got to hand it to him—he came up with a brilliant strategy for protecting himself and surviving his childhood. (Most of us do, in our own ways.) But it all came at a cost, setting up a major obstacle when it came to relationships, intimacy, and trust. Those old, unintegrated brain parts and that narrow, dry self-narrative had been running (and ruining) his relationships ever since.

By tuning in to Thomas's walled-off responses, I could hear the echoes of those deeply stored, untagged memories. It was a bit like listening for the tapping of survivors under the rubble of an earthquake.

In Thomas's case, it was pretty clear that his right hemisphere was the one buried. His left hemisphere, with all of its logic and language and linear thinking, was working just fine—but left and right weren't working well together. In addition, the feeling states that arise big-time in the lower levels of the brain, down in the recesses of the amygdala and among the rest of its limbic brethren, were getting smashed down by his higher-level, always rational cortex—almost like a big-brained bully, misguidedly "in service" to protect Thomas from his feelings.

So Thomas's work wasn't to take notes on scripted lines to say when his wife got on his case. It was to integrate his brain and get all the parts to do their stuff. Once he started moving more consistently toward integration, he would be better equipped to make greater sense of his life, of his responses, and of his relationships.

He wasn't sure he wanted to sign on for all that. Understandably, he didn't want to let go of his long-standing protective "academic" approach. Couldn't I just tell him what the problem was, tell him what to do and what to say?

That would be like picking the head off of a dandelion, but leaving the roots and leaves intact. The lawn might look better for a day or two, but it wasn't going to create lasting change. Thomas needed to be able to develop more tolerance for looking inside, and he needed to wire up a more integrated brain so he could stop being held hostage by his old relationship habits.

We spent more time in the next couple of sessions talking about his brain, about how thoughts are neuro-events, and how he could rewire his brain so that he'd know, himself, what to do, what to say. He warmed up to the idea somewhat, but wasn't ready to "sit and contemplate my navel." We continued to talk about his growing up, and his observations of his own baby boy, gradually shedding some light on the dusty old boxes in the attic and, along the way, giving him some safe experiences of having someone being attuned to him.

Guess Who Came to Dinner?

At the beginning of our fifth session, Thomas told me that his parents had come for a visit the previous weekend, to meet Thomas's son, Robert—their first grandbaby. I asked him what he'd noticed in seeing his parents with his son.

"It was rather strange. Veronica [his wife] noticed how completely awkward and uncomfortable my father looked when he was holding Robert—she said to me later that it looked as though he'd never held a baby before, even though there were four of us kids growing up. It kind of . . . surprised me. Knocked the wind out of me a little bit. I asked my mother if Dad had changed diapers, that kind of thing, and she said that my father just never did *any* 'hands-on' stuff with us. That was pretty crappy to hear, that he didn't even want to touch us."

And how was his mom with the baby? "She knew what to do, handled it in stride. Like when the baby woke up hungry, she'd go get his milk, seemed like she could tune out his crying, didn't seem to get irritated by it like my father did. She was even able to rig it so his bottle was propped up on some blankets and she could just sit in his room and look at a magazine while he drank his milk." He fell silent for a few moments, and he looked as though he were replaying that scene in his mind.

How'd that feel to see his mom in action? After a long pause, he said, "I appreciated my wife a lot more . . . I . . . guess I want my kid to get more than a propped-up bottle, y'know? Or a dad who—y'know—doesn't even want—can't even give the kid an actual goddamned hug." It was the first time I'd ever heard Thomas use anything even close to a curse-word. At this point, Thomas was looking down, picking a bit of lint from his pants. His eyes were reddened and moist; he sniffed, cleared his throat, and reached for a tissue. When I gently asked what was happening, he initially tried to dismiss it as a stuffy nose from allergies, but he looked up at me for just the briefest moment. I took a steady breath and stayed with Thomas, which seemed to allow him to stay with his feelings for just a second or two. He looked down, took a breath, and when he exhaled there was the sound of a sad sigh.

"I just . . . I want more for Robert. I want to be able to give him real damned hugs so he knows I love him."

When Thomas was ready, we eased in to exploring his attic, looking at many of the questions in the list below. It spurred and stirred him, and not just from a higher-cortical place. Together with the meditation exercise at the end of the chapter, he developed a bigger capacity to be with the feelings that came up as he talked about his answers.

Another important effect of the exploration and the exercise was that it was likely to help Thomas get his hippocampus online more, by increasing his ability to bring that helpful hippocampal "focused attention" and memory integration to bear on the here-and-now episodes and events of relationships and attachment—like with his wife and his baby boy. Getting emotional events to register consciously allows us to examine them, learn from them, and—you got it—make different choices based on our insight and self-awareness.

Self-Interview: Discovering the Elements of Your Story

The self-interview below can be helpful in developing a greater understanding of your own attachment history. It's meant to help you and your busy brain sit down long enough to shine some more light on some of the things that shaped your relationship style (and your brain). We can often do the equivalent of shorthand and random mumbling when we review our stories in our heads; putting pen to paper (or fingers to keyboard) supports a more coherent, and more useful, exploration. Take your time, and go at your own pace. This might be something that you complete over the course of an afternoon, or a month, or more. You might need to put it down for a while, to let things settle, before you pick it up again. Revisit your answers as more recollections—or data you get from others—come up.

Before you begin: Putting your experiences into words in a coherent way can help greatly with understanding yourself; it brings what might otherwise be "lurking" in the corners into a place where you can hold them with understanding and self-compassion. Dark attics and things that lurk can be scary, though. So, as with any exercise in which you might bump up against parts of yourself or your history that are painful or difficult, I encourage you to be gentle with yourself as you explore these questions. There's no award for being the toughest, or for going it alone—if it gets tough, consider seeking some good help, perhaps from a psychotherapist. (The Resources section may provide you with some leads.)

- What was your family like when you were young? (It may be helpful to divide this into different ages—for example, when you were in primary school, middle school, high school.)
- Who was in your family when you were growing up? Were there any other major players in your life back then—a teacher, a sitter, cousins who lived nearby, a neighbor? What was it like between you and each of those main characters? (It might be helpful to draw a sort of a "family tree" relationship diagram. Feel free to use colors, shapes, differently patterned lines to indicate the emotional connections—or lack thereof—between the branches and leaves.)
- Did the relationships in your family change as you grew older? (Again, drawing a diagram might help.)
- What was your father like? Are there ways in which you tried to be like him—or tried to be different from him? How about your mother?
- How did you learn how to "be" in the world? Did your parents use lectures; did they model the kinds of behavior they wanted you to learn? When you messed

up, what were their reactions like? How was discipline done? Do you think it had a positive effect on you, negative, or mixed?

- Do you recall times when you were separated from your parents? How old were you?
- Which emotions claimed the most room in your family when you were growing up—sadness? Joy? Anger? If one member of the family was having a strong emotional experience, how did other family members respond? Did their mood get "matched," ignored, shot down?
- How do you think your relationships growing up affect how your relationships are now, as an adult? Are there emotional or relationship habits you wish you'd never picked up? Any that you appreciate having learned?
- If you could wave your arm and change the way you think and feel about yourself, what, if anything, would you change? How about the way you relate to others?

Not long after his parents' visit, Thomas came in saying that he finally understood what his wife had been complaining about—if *he* hadn't known all these years what he was feeling, he could only imagine how frustrating and confusing it had been for her.

As he became more invested in being able to understand himself better, Thomas began to talk to other family members, and gathered some information that helped him understand his early years. One of his aunts told him that she remembered what a quiet, well-behaved baby he had always been, almost never crying, and always trying to be "so big and grown-up from the get-go." He also asked his friends about what it was like when they were growing up and had broken bones or gotten sick—and he felt "a bit surprised" again that the emotionally unresponsive stance of his parents was not, in fact, what his buddies had grown up with. He remarked that he felt lonely as he listened to his friends talk about their families, not because of what was going on here and now, but, he realized, because that's how he'd felt growing up. Lonely.

Thomas expanded his work outside the sessions to include jotting a brief note to himself when he noticed that he was in a dismissive or distant stance toward Veronica or little Robert (and gradually he was becoming open to Veronica's helping him notice these times). He set aside time each morning to look over those notes, and to reflect a bit on what implicit memories might have been tripping him up and sending him into that "unemotional" place.

Those morning times gradually became the time he committed to practicing basic mindfulness meditation. He started with just two minutes—an amount of time that he could tolerate, and in which he could also start to get some glimpses into his inner emotional life, beyond just his rational thoughts and judgments.

Over the course of the next few months, we talked about his understanding of how he had come to be a serious, cortically driven guy. He said, "I always thought I was just born that way, just a very levelheaded, evidence-based way of looking at everything. And that getting my parents' approval was the big prize, of course." He started to realize that maybe kids didn't have to "achieve" to be worthwhile. "Robert doesn't have to do anything to be amazing—he laughs after he sneezes, and Veronica and I both want to call the newspapers! It's a little ridiculous sometimes. But I look forward to coming home now. That's—well, that's not so ridiculous."

Thomas was looking more animated in our sessions. He said his wife was noticing that he played with Robert more and seemed more willing to do things with him—not only diapering him and carrying him on family outings, but occasionally getting goofy with the baby, playing and making faces. "This weekend we discovered a new game together. I'd make a frown, and Robert would get all serious, like this ultra-focused bald little CEO in a diaper. Then I'd start to do something, make a little silly noise or waggle my eyebrows, and his whole body lit up. It was like an electric current—I could feel it in mine, too—and just like that, we're both laughing." He paused, and then said with a small, little-kid smile, "Very, very cool."

BODY SCAN MEDITATION

For those of us who learned early on that the attic—the place where we stored our experiences, our stories—was a spooky or hazardous place, we need to stretch our ability to turn on the light and sit with the tangled mess of leftovers, useless junk, and garbage that's sometimes stored up there.

Being able to stretch that ability, to tolerate the feelings that come up—in meditation, or at other times—comes from practice. The meditation that follows will help you install a work light in your own attic.

This meditation is one that I've found to be helpful in improving communications between the body, the brain, and the mind—moving you toward greater capacity for self-knowing. When you come upon a feeling in your body, it's often linked to an old, implicit piece of your memory. Being better able to notice the sensations can be like following the trail of bread crumbs in Hansel and Gretel.

Your goal in this meditation is to bring your awareness to the sensations in your body. It isn't about separating from yourself and being an observer of your sensations; rather, you're in the sensory experience, feeling it and being aware of it. If you're focusing your awareness on your hand, feel from your hand, being in it rather than seeing it as an external object.

One of the common experiences in meditation practice is that we become aware of a sensation that is unpleasant (like tightness in our chest or belly). Our tendency is to go immediately from experiencing the discomfort to assuming that something is wrong—we go to fear. Most of the time, though, there's nothing seriously wrong, and if we can increase our capacity to just let it be, without immediate reactivity, we gain an amazing perspective, and sometimes we come to a greater understanding of what's been dwelling in there for years. This serves us incredibly well when it comes to relationships. One harsh look from your partner may give rise to a tightness in your gut, an old reaction built on old experiences. Just because your gut is tight, you don't need to fight or flee. You can have a more open curiosity about it. So, as you practice this meditation, know that you are enhancing your ability to be present and aware, remaining open, and shedding some compassionate light in your attic.

One more note: sometimes, beginning to notice more about your inner experience can bring up feelings that might feel like "too much." This can be especially true if you have a history that includes trauma. As I've noted before, in this meditation, and in all mindfulness exercises, please be sure to be compassionate with yourself, and stop if you start to feel flooded by your feelings or overwhelmed in any way. Talking to someone who can help you with these issues may need to come first, before you embark on a practice of meditation. I've included resources and suggestions for finding help at the end of the book.

Following the same process as in the Basic Mindfulness Meditation Instructions, settle in comfortably to your seat, close or soften your eyes, and bring your awareness to your breath. Allow your breath's own natural rhythm to settle in.

Gently, and with an open awareness, guide your attention to the top of your head. Encourage yourself to do this without using your eyes, without an imagined view of the top of your head; rather, feel the top of your head from within yourself. You're not looking for anything in particular, just becoming aware of any sensations there. You might notice an itch, or some tightness, or other sensations. All sensations are just fine, and you can simply notice them and let them be. You might, like many people, feel nothing there at all, and that's fine too. Allow your awareness to linger there for just a while longer, enlarging your capacity to be open to whatever your body experiences or doesn't experience in the moment.

Move into an open and relaxed scan of your body's sensations, flowing from the top of your head down the back and sides of your head and on to your ears. At whatever pace and depth you like, bring your awareness to your forehead and your eyes; your nose, your cheeks, and your jaw. When you're ready, guide your awareness to your mouth: the outside, around your lips; the sensations you experience where your lips meet or part; inside, the top and bottom of your tongue, the roof of your mouth.

Whenever images, thoughts, memories, and so on come up, gently remind yourself that this kind of wandering is natural, and gently bring your awareness back to the sensations in your body at this moment.

Continue guiding your awareness as you scan down from your mouth into your neck and throat. Invite yourself to see whatever sensations are there. Move into your shoulders, first each shoulder, then the areas between them on your upper back and on your upper chest. Your focus is on the experience from inside, as the experiencer rather than the observer.

Slowly and gently move your awareness down into your arms; your upper arms and forearms; then into your wrists and hands. As you shift your awareness into your fingers, and then each finger, you might notice your pulse or the slight sensation of pressure where your fingers are resting. Simply notice.

Whenever you find your awareness adrift in thoughts, simply and gently notice that it has happened (*thinking . . . thinking*) and, without judgment, kindly and softly bring your awareness back to the sensations in your body.

When you feel ready, continue your scan in your chest and around to your upper back; down into your middle and lower back, and gradually through your back to your belly. Rest your awareness there, feeling the sensations inside and on your skin. Gently invite your awareness to move into your hips, your buttocks. Again, as the experiencer, guide your awareness of sensations into your genitals, your upper legs. What are the sensations in your knees, your calves, your shins? At your preferred pace, move into your ankles, your feet, and your toes, and sense what there is to sense.

If it feels right to you, now bring your awareness into a larger focus, still from within, as the experiencer rather than the observer, becoming aware of your whole body's sensory experience. Gently hold your awareness there, without hunting for or pushing away any of the sensations. If you notice a particular sensation, be open to it, let it rise and fall and shift, simply experiencing it.

Feel free to vary the way you do the body scan from session to session. Sometimes you might move through the scan more than once in a session; other times, you might do one full scan, find one area of your body with sensations that are asking for more attention, and practice there for a while longer. Whatever helps you feel more aware of the sensations in your body will help you improve communications between the body, the brain, and the mind, making you more available for healthy, attuned, conscious relationships.

CHAPTER 8

ACQUIRING A VOLTMETER

Empathy

Insight into your own inner workings, and having a coherent narrative about how you came to be you, are incredibly important for healthy relationships—and when you put those together with being empathic?

Wow.

Now you got it goin' *on.*

Like lots of other people, for too many years I had empathy all wrong. Okay, well, to be more self-empathic, I only had it partly wrong, but it was an important part. Vital, even.

Mostly, I thought being empathic was about tuning in to others, getting what they were feeling. And then, to the very best of my ability, it was my task to try to make everyone feel better.

It worked, in a lot of ways. When I was little, I was really good at being able to detect the mood of my mother and behave in ways that I knew would make her feel better. I figured out how to soothe my dad's ruffled feathers after my mother had dissed him.

Without consciously realizing it, I'd taken as fact that, *if only I tried hard enough,* I could make everybody feel better. If they didn't feel better, I felt like a failure—or, to put it in attachment terms, I was afraid that they'd no longer love me.

And boy-howdy, did I try. Remember how I mentioned before that I had anxious insomnia when I was ten? Yep. That came from trying so hard to make everyone okay, from all of that "empathizing."

Apparently, I didn't get the memo that "everyone" included *me. I* was miserable.

I ended up being a kind of mind-reader/doormat, trying to come to everyone's emotional rescue. My mother (for whom empathy was not a strong suit) was both mystified and disgusted by how I seemed to be thrilled that high-school friends constantly came to me with their problems. "Why on earth would you ever want to be crawling around in other people's emotional underwear?"

Learning well and thoroughly from my early experiences with my primary caregivers—well-meaning parents who hadn't figured enough out about their own attachment *shtick*—"attachment" for me meant that I had to give myself up and please the other person in order to have someone who was willing to be there for me.

I eventually figured out that being empathic isn't about being an all-absorbing antenna, a doormat, a mind reader, and/or an emotional rescuer. It's also not about fear (as in the fear of being alone, having someone be mad at you, disappointing someone, and so on). Being able to understand another person's state of mind—using an emotional voltmeter—is essential for healthy relationships, but being able to do so without losing your awareness of your own state of mind is vitally important. It's also something that mindfulness develops and supports extremely well, as you'll see.

Dogs Do It

Empathy, as it turns out, isn't a uniquely human trait or ability. At the entry level, it's "the ability to be affected by and share the emotional state of another being" (as renowned primatologist Frans de Waal, PhD, thinks of it). Anyone who's ever loved a dog knows what I'm talking about—if you're happy, the dog's happy. If you're blue, the dog's blue. This is the ground floor of empathy.

This first level of empathy isn't even something we decide to do. It's an automatic, involuntary activity that starts in the body. You detect what others are feeling, and before you can even register it consciously, you feel it. Period. Before you even know it.

It's a "blind" reading, rather than an integrated, useful, feedback-producing voltmeter.

Hook people up to some electrodes designed to measure their facial responses, then subliminally flash facial expressions on a computer screen they're watching. Even when the images flash so quickly that they're below the threshold of conscious awareness, the subjects' facial muscles will match the expressions on the screen. Simple mimicry? Apparently not—because if you ask subjects afterward to rate how they feel, the ones whom you've subliminally exposed to smiling faces say they feel good. And the ones to whom you've shown the frowning faces feel worse.

Congratulations! You've just entered the first level of empathy: *emotional contagion*. Sounds kind of gross, like catching some nasty skin disease, and, as a kid and young adult, it did feel like I was mucking about in the sewers much of the time, sucked in there without even realizing it, feeling other people's feelings and often confusing them with my own.

Emotional contagion's a useful thing, really it is. Take, for example, a herd of zebras. One of them notices a lion—that zebra's emotional state of arousal and alarm spreads throughout the herd like lightning. None of the zebras pause, stand pensively with hoof to temple, and muse, "Gee, I wonder if Phil's got a gas bubble or if we're all about to be eaten?" One zebra feels it, and very quickly they all feel it, automatically activating their evasive maneuvers before becoming lunch.

Pigeons, mice, birds, monkeys, dogs—human infants—they're all scoring well on this basic level of empathy. They've got some of the basic brain and nervous-system parts up and working, including areas that can detect things like changes in posture and behavior.

Since I'm fairly confident that you're not a zebra, I'm going to have you imagine your human self walking around at a festive gathering of other humans. From across the room, you see a group of other humans you know and trust, and you see them laughing. You smile, and maybe you even feel yourself tickled in your belly, too. Tag! You've been emotionally contaminated!

Or you're in a pretty good mood when your partner comes home from work. She has a tight look on her face, her jaw is clenched, and her briefcase gets plunked a little too firmly on the floor. Your facial muscles shift immediately and there's a tightness in your stomach. Tag again!

But simply being able to catch someone else's emotion, like some kind of instant-acting germ, isn't really what we're aiming for. Let's kick it up a notch, and get more of your brain in the game. You want to be more empathic than a pigeon, don't you?

I Understand

Sympathetic concern is the next level of empathy. You start with emotional contagion, then add a capacity to appraise the other's situation and to try to understand why they're feeling the way they do. De Waal calls this "cognitive empathy"—you're putting some thought into it, not just reacting at an automatic, bodily level.

This is also the level at which *consoling* starts to kick in. If you see your partner coming in the door looking tight and upset, you experience the emotional contagion (you feel some of her distress and alarm in your own body) *and* you can try to figure out why she's in such a worked-up state—you might also then be able to consider the best ways to console her based on her current emotional needs.

Unlike the zebra, you're not just feeling your partner's distress, but you're also figuring out what you might do to alleviate some of it. You might soften your face and ask empathically about what's up. You might put your arm around her.

Monkeys are capable of showing this level of sympathetic concern, and of consoling one another (one monkey might console the loser of a fight, for example, by putting his arm around him). But it appears (from Frans de Waal's point of view, as one example) that they're doing this because, as they experience the emotional contagion of the loser, *they* feel yucky inside, and in order to alleviate their own yucky feelings, they try to get their tribe-mate to feel better so they can feel better too.

Been there, done that. Not where I wanted to stay. How about you? Ready to take it to the next level? You made it past the pigeons—want to make it past monkeys now?

Get steady and grounded, because you're going to need to be in two places at once: having a sense of your self and simultaneously being able to take the perspective of the other.

Standing in Their Shoes—with Feeling

Empathic perspective taking is the next level. For a lot of people, "perspective taking" is what it means to be empathic—identifying with the other and being able to see things from someone else's experience.

But—you could do that without actually *feeling* much. You can see this in intellectual debates: in order to argue against your opponent effectively, you need to be able to intellectually understand his or her point of view in order to effectively tear it down. From this stance, you can get into the head of the other person and get the cognitive perspective, then explain your perspective from an equally intellectual, cognitive stance. Okay on the debate team, but not so hot in your relationship. You end up missing out on what's going on emotionally for your significant other, who says, "You just don't get it!!" From your side, you're pretty clear that you do, in *fact* (and I emphasize that word for a reason), "get it," but you get it only intellectually. So you think your significant other is being irrational. And your significant other *is* being "irrational," thank goodness—if we were nothing but rational, we'd be robots.

Feelings and emotions aren't rational thoughts. They aren't meant to be. They provide a balance to the rational, and as such they follow a different path. They bring color and life and vibrancy to our existence. They come from a different part of the brain, and they're important, vital, and too often disrespected, much to our detriment. If you're going to "get it," you've got to "get" the emotional connection as well.

Taken to its extreme, if you excelled at perspective taking but couldn't do it at all from an empathic place, you'd make an excellent psychopath—able to understand how other people think, getting their state of mind, without feeling it yourself. No empathy, just perspective taking. You'd be really good at knowing how to torture somebody.

Most people who are in this rational, intellectual approach to relationships aren't psychopaths at all. They're simply responding to the world from a protective stance, probably learned early on, which we talked about earlier as "avoidant attachment." *Emotions are these unpredictable and potentially painful things that weren't safe when I was a kid, so I've learned to take a detour around them as often as possible.*

And then there's a counterpart to that stance, the path of many who have a tendency toward anxious attachment. Sometimes the folks in this category are *too* good at tuning in to and feeling what their partners (or friends or co-workers) are feeling, so much so that their own experiences and perspectives get lost. They often are so very busy taking care of the needs of others that they eventually start to crumble—or get resentful, angry, depressed, burned out, maybe even physically sick.

If this sounds like you, you probably learned to do it this way so early and so well that your brain—which, you'll remember, wires itself in response to what you do with it most often—might just go blank when you even try to consider doing things differently. Or when you *do* try to stay on your own side more, you ditch all empathy and just start acting angry and selfish, like a pendulum that was stuck all the way to one side, now knocked loose and lodged on the other extreme of its arc.

To be empathic, you need to be able to tune in to someone else, "get" what his or her experience is, and yet not lose yourself in the deal.

Wait a Minute— What *Is* Attunement, Anyway?

Let's focus a bit more on this ability to tune in to someone else. Attunement is one of the necessary ingredients for a fully developed ability to be empathic.

It's probably easiest to break attunement down into three chunks:

1. **Basic definition:** Attunement is the "taking in" of the internal state of another person and then having that shape your own internal state.
2. **The experience of attunement:** When you're attuned, there's a sense of "getting" what someone else is feeling—often, in your gut, as in "Whoa, I got that!" It's a deeply felt sense of connection that is as much about the other person as it is about you. When you're tuned in to someone else, he or she might experience "feeling felt" by you.
3. **What's going on in your body and brain:** By tuning in, you're "taking in" to your own nervous system the other person's internal world. You are perceiving not only what the person is saying, but also the eye contact between you, the other person's facial expression (including subtleties that you're not even consciously

aware of, like pupil size), and physiological signs like breathing, the relative tightness of the jaw, tone of voice, movements (hands, arms, head), posture, and the size and timing of responses. And you're feeling it in your own body, like a "feeling mirror"—most of the time without even knowing it. In fact, we automatically and involuntarily mimic the facial expressions of others. There's even a recent study that looked at what happens if your own facial muscles are "dampened" by the injection of Botox—those who received the injection were significantly worse at reading the facial emotions of others.[1] Having a good body-sense awareness allows you to be much better at gathering here-and-now info.

So How Do We Tune In and Feel Empathy?

There's still a lot of research that needs to be done about the neurobiology of empathy—how we come to know the internal state of the other and not get it confused with our own. We don't know as much as we'd like to about how empathy "happens" in the brain. Currently, there are two leading possibilities—two different kinds of brain cells that, oddly enough, don't seem to be related to one another. Let's take a look at them each in turn.

Wired for Empathy Possibility #1: Mirror Neurons. The first very cool but still murky possibility is that special neurons found in various areas of the brain, dubbed *mirror neurons,* might be part of what affords us the capacity for "feeling you, feeling me, getting you."

Mirror neurons have their skeptics. For one thing, it's unclear—and difficult to measure directly—whether they exist in humans (they were first noted in macaque monkeys). For another, it's still debated whether they do what some researchers claim they do. And, if they do exist in humans, we don't know all the possible places in the brain they might exist. (Again, it's because of the difficulty in measuring them—at the ideal level, it involves sticking electrodes into the brain and measuring responses from individual neurons. I'm not signing up for that experiment, are you?)

Okay, so if mirror neurons do exist, what are they doing? The notion is that they get turned on by seeing someone else do something—specifically, doing something *with intention.*

The example often used is of licking an ice-cream cone (because that's what evoked the firing in the macaques' mirror neurons the first time it was accidentally observed—a researcher had walked into the lab with some gelato. Ah, science). If all you're doing is standing about and sticking your tongue in and out, without *intention,* the mirror neurons in my brain would not be expected to fire in response.

But if you're doing that same mouth-tongue thing to the gelato in your hand, my mirror neurons would reportedly fire up in response.

And—here's the wild part—the neurons that then fire in *my* brain are the same neurons that are firing in *your* brain as *you're* doing it—it's as if I'm doing your "licking with intention" in my own brain. This could mean that, in the example of your partner coming in the door and slamming her briefcase down, mirror neurons allow information to flow and reverberate like this:

1. Your mirror neurons, which are possibly located in certain parts of your cortex (upper brain), are activated by the observation of your partner's actions. The mirror neurons send signals to other areas, including (possibly) an area that helps you tap into memory and experience and anticipate what your partner might do next—to understand her intention.
2. The information from the mirror neurons is also being processed in your insula—which, you'll remember, is sometimes called the "limbic integration cortex."
3. The insula sends the info from the mirror neurons down to the limbic areas (at least, that's what's suggested by research from the lab at UCLA run by Marco

Iacoboni, MD, PhD[2]), and your amygdala gets in on the act to decide "threat or no threat."

4. Depending on how the amygdala interprets it, your body responds—your face might get tight, and your gut might clench, for example, in response to your limbic system deciding, "Bad things are happening."
5. The information about what's going on in your partner and is now also going on in your body is sent the other way, upward, from the back of the insula to the front, and on up to the middle prefrontal cortex.
6. Now's your big chance—the chance for conscious, higher-level processing about all of this body sensation and feelings and stuff! Now you can make the assessment of "Well, then, what's caused this uncomfortable state?"
7. Depending on how grounded you are in knowing yourself and your history, and how well you regulate your bodily and emotional responses:
    - You might get it right (*maybe that review with her boss today went really badly*), or
    - Your bias might botch it for you (*she's mad at me because everyone's always mad at me because I'm a wretch*).

Mirror neurons, if they indeed exist and if they inform empathy in humans, might learn from experience, which would be good—you could know what to make of it when someone is extending a knife toward you when you're cooking together in the kitchen, as opposed to when you're walking down a dark street.

But if you've got a history that has taught your mirror neurons to expect that others routinely harm you (in the case of abuse, for example), you might always react with alarm and make an assumption of intended harm whenever you see someone so much as look at a knife in your presence, regardless of the context or their intention.

Wired for Empathy Possibility #2: von Economo Neurons. I find myself enamored with von Economo neurons (VENs) more than mirror neurons when it comes to my own "SWAG"* about the neurological underpinnings of the "higher" levels of empathy.

Here are a few of the reasons why VENs might woo you, too. First, VENs seem to get busy when we're distinguishing between our self and another. As it turns out, developing the capacity to discriminate between what's "you" and what's "someone else"—a necessary ability for self-awareness and accurate attunement—exists only in certain mammals: some whales, bottlenose dolphins, elephants, and the great apes. (The great apes include chimpanzees, bonobos, orangutans, gorillas, and you and me—assuming we're both adult humans.)

So far, these are the only animals in which VENs have been found. Not only do the animals in the elite VEN club all have that capacity, they also all have a prolonged juvenile stage where they learn from (and are nurtured by) their elders—early attuned attachment, perhaps? I find this intriguing.

And—you might have guessed this—these are also the only animals that have been found to be capable of perspective taking. Mm-hmm.

VENs have only been found thus far in some regions with which you're already familiar: the anterior cingulate cortex (ACC), part of the anterior insula, and a part of the prefrontal cortex (specifically, the dorsolateral prefrontal cortex), all important structures in the relationship brain.

* "Scientific Wild Ass Guess"

Mirror Neurons and VENs and . . . We Don't Know

So, at the cellular level, the chief "empathy suspects" are von Economo neurons (found in the ACC, anterior insula, and part of the prefrontal cortex) and mirror neurons (or a mirror system). Which means that we have some fascinating leads on what allows our brains to afford us the glorious capacity for full-on empathy, but we have a lot of work still to be done.

What we think we *do* know about the brain, the body, and empathy is this: Empathy requires an integration of information coming in from the outside (from your partner, the context, etc.) and information about what you're experiencing. Once you've integrated the info, you then generate a hypothesis about what's "going on" in your partner.

We do have to remember, though, that we all have a library of expectations and at-the-ready internal responses, which we've accumulated throughout our history—and these can distort and contaminate our ability to accurately attune to what is actually going on, what the other person's internal state is, and what his or her intentions are. They can also distort our capacity to be empathic.

To be accurately attuned, you need to be able to start from the actual information in the moment—like a good detective, you need to perceive and be open to what the evidence is telling you, rather than what you want (or need) the evidence to be.

The brain-structure areas that we suspect of playing a role in empathy include your prefrontal cortex (more specifically, the inferior or "lower" frontal cortex); your insula (more specifically, the front or anterior part of the insula); your anterior cingulate cortex (ACC); and your limbic areas, including the amygdala—which need to be online but not over-reactive, of course—along with the body areas that respond automatically to others, such as the gut, heart, and facial muscles.

Playing on All Levels

While we still have only initial clues about what's going on in the brain and body when it comes to empathy, it does seem to be the case that, for the highest level of empathy, you need the following elements, which we discussed above:

- **Level 1—Emotional contagion:** The bodily capacity for "state matching"—the ability to be affected by "emotional contagion"
- **Level 2—Sympathetic concern:** The capacity to assess why someone else might be feeling what they're feeling and to effectively offer consolation
- **Level 3—Empathic perspective taking:** The capacity to:
  - adopt the perspective of another;
  - offer help that's informed by the other's perspective; and
  - do (a) and (b) without losing your own sense of self.

All three levels are necessary. Skipping a level doesn't work—at least, not if your purpose is to be in a healthy relationship.

Wired for Empathy, *But* . . .

Bottom line: we've got some highly specialized wiring for empathy, even if we don't understand it yet.

Of course, that doesn't mean that we're wired *only* for empathy—we're capable of many experiences in response to others, including hostile aggression, selfishness, and competitiveness, just to name a few.

So how do we increase our chances of being empathic in a given situation with our partners?

How do we shift the likelihood in favor of being able to "do" all of these highly integrated events that allow us to be empathic instead of jerks—or doormats?

Hmmm, what if you could do something that's being shown to increase empathy, improve body awareness, create a larger and more connected insula and anterior cingulate, quell the limbic areas . . .

You know where I'm headed with this: mindfulness practice. It's one of your best shots at beefing up your insula, ACC, prefrontal and limbic areas—all the regions we have a good guess are involved in empathy.

Wire up a better voltmeter, and practice plugging it in and accurately reading it.

LOVING-KINDNESS MEDITATION

The meditation practice described below is called a *mettâ* practice. *Mettâ* translates roughly as "loving-kindness" from Pâli (a Sanskrit dialect, the language in which the oral teachings of Buddha were first written down).

Mettâ isn't a practice that will make you all mushy and wishy-washy and so loving and kind toward others that you end up turning into a warm asphalt highway for all the 18-wheelers in your life.

Rather, this practice, from the perspective of your brain and your body, will help you develop an awareness of the "voltage" in others while also being tuned in to your own voltage. It helps you make a healthier distinction between yourself and others, without the habit of doing it by selfishness or creating stone walls in your heart.

In this mettâ practice, you're going to be *practicing the intention for well-being* in yourself, then going through a list of others for whom you also hold this intention. To yourself and others, you'll be sending loving, positive intentions such as *May you know peace* and *May you be happy.*

Practicing mettâ meditation often seems like one of the easiest practices for new meditators, because it has specific things for you to be thinking about—but while your thoughts during mettâ are somewhat more guided than in some other practices, it's not about rote instruction following. It's about paying *attention to the intention* of a heart and body experience of loving-kindness. If you find that all you're doing is running through the script, you've missed the mark.

To paraphrase George Carlin, "Ya gotta *wanna*."[3] Now, fully allowing yourself to be aware of and intent upon feelings of love and kindness for yourself *and* for others is not what most people would call easy. So—and here's the challenging part—as you experience difficulties with this, *offer empathy to yourself.* Tara Brach, PhD, instructs in *Radical Acceptance,* "Even if you do not immediately feel [it], your willingness alone can reconnect you to your loving heart."[4]

Ronald Siegel, PsyD, in *The Mindfulness Solution,* talks about "affectionate awareness." As you practice mettâ, you (being human, with all those competing needs and thoughts and feelings) will inevitably find yourself not only with a wandering mind—but oh, boy, you're also going to bump into a not-so-loving-kindness mind! The object isn't to slap a happy-face sticker over all of your feelings in order to radiate nothing but Love throughout the meditation. Your *intention* here is really what "counts" (although no one's keeping score).

This is one of the places where people who tend to want to make others happy—but end up getting lost in the process—can get twisted tighter than a tornado. You can't make someone else happy, well, or peaceful, but you might be vulnerable to getting sucked into trying. So, here, you get to practice staying with yourself—with your awareness of your own body—and to remember the wise words of Sharon Salzberg:

> The intention is enough. . . . We form the *intention* in our mind for our happiness and the happiness of all. This is different from struggling to fabricate a certain feeling, to create it out of our will, to make it happen. We just settle back and plant the seeds without worrying about the immediate result.[5]

There was one morning, after I'd started regular mettâ practice, that I remember well. I had a big day ahead of me, but hey, I'd been meditating pretty regularly for a while, and I was definitely better at handling stress without getting amygdala-hijacked.

But on this particular morning, my darling husband was having a rough time. He was grumpy, he was overloaded with too many responsibilities and too little sleep, and he was just in an obviously miserable, grouchy place.

I tried to be empathic. I tried to figure out what was wrong. I tried to cheer him up. I tried . . . well, I tried too hard. And he still wasn't responding.

So I got mad. I gave myself up and got sucked into his grumpiness. My limbic brain got busy being pissy, but it was wrestling with another part of my brain that was trying to do better. I'd just practiced my meditation, after all—who did he think he was messing with my mettâ?!

With my now clenched jaw and a deep, menacing growl in my voice, I looked at him and snarled, "May you know peace"—one of the statements from mettâ practice.

He laughed. Bless his heart, he laughed. He laughed so hard he spewed coffee out of both mouth *and* nose, and then we were both standing there laughing so hard we could barely breathe.

A few notes before you begin:

- In this practice, you're going to be bringing to mind different people. It's most helpful not to choose people who hold a particularly romantic or sexual charge for you (or who you think should do so), such as your spouse, partner, or secret crush.
- I find it best to focus on those who are living. I've found that it's not as helpful (though it can be easier) to generate loving-kindness for those who can no longer annoy us.
- I also advise that you steer clear of bringing to mind people with whom you are having or have had intense or destructive connections, at least until you are much better grounded in your ability to hold on to yourself.
- Keep in mind that this practice isn't intended to work through complex issues such as previous trauma. You may want to enlist the help of a good psychotherapist if you think you might encounter feelings that seem overwhelming or too frightening.

First, settle into your body as in the Basic Mindfulness Meditation Instructions at the end of Chapter 3.

Now, bring your awareness to having a feeling of calm kindness. It might help to be aware of softening the muscles around your eyes and imagining your mouth having an inward smile. I find it very helpful to place my hand over my heart (really on my heart, in the middle of my chest, not the polite place you might put your hand when reciting the Pledge of Allegiance).

Starting with yourself, focus your intention on sending out several positive, caring feelings—for example:

May I be free.

May I be peaceful and at ease.

May I be happy.

May I be safe.

The exact words aren't important; choose phrases that feel right to you—although, as Sharon Salzberg points out, it's better if it's something "deeply felt and somewhat enduring (not something like 'May I find a good show on television tonight')."[6] As you slowly and gently direct these intentions, feel in your heart, in your belly, on your face, in your breath, your intention of loving-kindness. You're aware of what your body is experiencing as you have these feelings and these thoughts.

And when—not if—you find your mind wandering, consider adding the phrase, "May I be kind to myself."

Now practice directing these intentions toward the people listed below, each in turn, settling into each as you go. With the same sweet patience you might have for that puppy we talked about in the meditation instructions at the end of Chapter 3, gently remind yourself, as your mind wanders off, or as your empathy takes a detour, to return your awareness to your intentions and to the feelings in your body.

- **A mentor, a teacher, a benefactor.** Choose someone who's been kind and generous with you. It could be someone in your life now or someone from your past. It can even be someone whom you've never met—some people find it helpful to bring to mind a leader whom they respect and have learned much from. The only suggestion here is to choose someone who is not your spouse, not your lover, but still someone for whom you can easily generate a feeling of warmth and care. Again, feel a sense of loving-kindness toward this person, and bring your awareness to what is taking place in your heart, your belly, and on your face. While you hold this person in your heart, repeat the phrases you said for yourself—*May I be free. May I be peaceful and at ease,* and so on—replacing "I" with "you": *May you be free. May you be peaceful and at ease . . .*

- **An acquaintance.** Next, choose a "neutral" person—someone you might encounter often, such as the hostess in your neighborhood coffee shop, but whom you don't know well, who evokes neither particularly positive nor particularly negative feelings. Again, holding this person in your heart, repeat your wishes of loving-kindness toward him or her.

- **A person with whom you've had some difficulty.** At first, it might be best to choose someone who isn't heavily loaded in your experience (as noted above, steer clear of those who have been destructive or intensely troublesome until you have a lot more practice and grounding under your belt). Repeat your wishes of mettâ while holding that person in your heart. When you begin to feel yourself losing your intention of loving-kindness here, welcome to the club! Forgive yourself, and allow yourself to return to someone "easy" until you feel grounded in your awareness and intention again.

- **A group of people of which you're a part.** Choose, for example, the people who work on the same floor of your office building; your neighbors; your church community; the city or state in which you live. You could follow the classic instructions and go for "every sentient being in the universe," but please remember to be kind to yourself. Don't try to heal the world all at once, all on your own.

Use this group as the focus of your loving-kindness phrase repetition.

- **Back to yourself.** Returning to loving-kindness of yourself before ending formal mettâ practice, I find, is important in bringing you back to including yourself in your capacity for empathy. So, as your final part of this meditation, repeat the phrases with yourself as the focus—*May I be free. May I be peaceful and at ease. May I be happy. May I be safe.*

CHAPTER 9

We're All on the Same Power Grid

From *Me* to *We*

Having a psychotherapy office that's a four-minute cab ride from the White House and basically next door to K Street where the nation's most powerful lobbying firms abound, I sometimes see patients who are "persons of power"—who influence and impact the lives of millions of people they'll never even meet.

Justine was just such a person.

In her late 40s, Justine had already been a senior aide to more than one powerful legislator on Capitol Hill, a mover and shaker in driving prominent national campaigns, and she was considered one of the 50 most powerful lobbyists in the city.

When she called for her first appointment, she said she was frustrated about being unable to find a relationship. "There just aren't any decent men out there."

Her first session was a little bumpy. She was 15 minutes late, due to a pressing matter on the Hill, and she insisted that she needed to leave her BlackBerry on so she could check to see if anything urgent came up.

Justine told me the problem was that there were simply no good, smart, single men in D.C. who seemed capable of dating a powerful woman who earned more than they did. As she spoke, she didn't come across as vain or egotistical—she wasn't telling me about her status to impress me. She seemed sad and frustrated.

She'd apparently dated quite a bit, but the way she described it, most of them had fallen into one of two categories: "Lying Liars" or "Wimpy Boys." She repeated the lament she'd made in her initial phone call: "There just aren't any decent guys out there."

The majority of the guys she'd dated, she reported, were guys who lied about whether or not they were really (*really*) divorced, about the important people they knew, how many other women they were dating at the same time, how much money they made, how much time they spent looking at online porn, and on and on.

Then there were a few guys who'd been "total wimps"—couldn't handle her busy schedule; were intimidated by her power, her salary, her house, et cetera; went along with anything she said and had no opinions of their own; and "didn't seem to know who they wanted to be when they grew up. I mean, these are men in their 40s, for f*@#'s sake!"

So, she concluded, "There just really aren't any good men around. How am I supposed to find a decent relationship?"

(Side note: The Washington, D.C., metro area has a population of more than five million people, at last count. And there are plenty of single men who don't fall into Justine's two categories.)

Over the next few sessions, Justine talked quite a lot about her work. Her BlackBerry kept it ever present, buzzing and alarming and demanding her attention.

She described the wheeling and dealing, the way she'd use her connections and leverage and charm to get people to see things her way—or rather, her client's way. Most of the time, she said, she thought that what she was doing for her clients was on the up and up, but pretty distasteful when it came to policy.

Meaning that on a daily basis, from breakfast meetings through late-night meetings over pricey scotch, she was advocating for things she didn't believe in. Often, they were things that she knew were actually pretty bad for most people, but good for her huge corporate clients. She knew lawmakers who were involved in questionable deals, she chummed with fellow lobbyists whom she knew to be engaging in unethical practices, and she was privy to a ridiculous number of affairs. Justine also had high blood pressure, and when I asked her about how she dealt with the stress of her job, she said, "Oh, I self-medicate with a little too much to drink."

This, from a girl raised in a hardworking Midwestern farm family whose grandfather was a minister—as she put it, "not one of those sleazy televangelists, either—he's the real deal. Eighty-seven years old, but rock-solid in body, mind, and spirit. Poor as dirt, though. I send money home to him and my grandmother, but he ends up giving it to someone he thinks needs it more. That kind of guy."

She liked her job, she said; it was exciting and stimulating. "I just have to separate out the downsides in my mind—it's just what I do for my clients. It's not who I am. Plus, it pays outrageously well, so I can give plenty of money to charities I really believe in—to balance things out a little—and still live in a fabulous house."

The only thing missing, she said, was that she wanted a partner. A husband.

I asked Justine what her minister grandfather thought of her work. She laughed. "Well, let's just say that he prays for me. And I haven't even told him most of it!" She also wondered about whether the reason her grandfather never used the money she sent, but gave it to others, was "because maybe he thinks of it as 'tainted.' I don't do anything illegal in my work. I follow all the rules and regulations. He just thinks that I should be using my power to serve the Lord instead of Big Business. He . . . he thinks what I do is immoral and self-centered."

I asked her what she thought. "Well, like I said, it's all legal. But I do have those moments when I think I'll just save enough to retire early and then do something that's not just making rich people richer."

Uncomfortably Numb

On an almost hourly basis, 12 to 15 hours a day, Justine was doing and saying things that, by her own description, went against her grain. She knew that some of what her grandfather said was true—that there was a fair amount of unjust, unfair, and/or mercenary decision-making that she was a big part of. But, she said, she'd learned to "separate it out," to tune out the feeling that what she was doing on behalf of her client was wrong. "They hire me to do a job, and I do it. Like a defense attorney representing somebody he knows is guilty."

How do we make decisions about what's important to ourselves and what's self-centered to the point of being destructive to others? And what guides our choice of action? That's a thorny question, and it goes well beyond the scope of our discussion here, but in terms of how we do our relationships—with ourselves, with others to whom we're close, and with the broader community—it's helpful to understand a least a bit of how the brain seems to process the question of what's the right thing to do. Do you choose from the perspective of your individual self ("me"), your closest kin ("mine"), your community ("us"), and so on—or everyone with whom you share the planet?

At what point does "me" become "we"? When does "us" begin to include "them"?

We are, after all, increasingly interconnected, so any choices we make are bound to affect not only our lives, but also the lives of those around us. This means that—to live true to ourselves—our choices need to take into consideration the fact that we are part of a larger whole. Even though he was talking about the Cold War, President John F. Kennedy's words from 1963 are just as apt, if not more so, today:

> In the final analysis, our most basic common link is that we all inhabit this small planet. We all breathe the same air. We all cherish our children's future. And we are all mortal.[1]

Believing, as many of us do, that higher reasoning and sound judgment are the result of our highly developed neocortex, we also tend to believe that when decision making takes into account larger and broader implications, it comes from that higher-level thinking as well. Thinking about the impact of our own choices on the broader community is abstract, and therefore it comes from parts of the brain that form abstract, conscious thoughts, such as the prefrontal cortex. According to this "neocortex theory of social development" (not a real name), that's why little kids make selfish decisions, but as we grow and learn and our prefrontal cortex develops, we make decisions that take others into account, that serve the greater good.

Let's look at that rationalist perspective a little more closely. The research that most closely hews to this type of decision making is the investigation of moral choices.

If people are asked about the morality of a brother and sister having sex with each other (the story presented in one study by Jonathan Haidt, PhD, professor at the University of Virginia[2])—most of them will label it morally wrong. When asked why they find it immoral, though, they run into some trouble. They'll come up with reasons, such as the genetic dangers for children of close relatives, or tell you that having sex with your sibling could be emotionally damaging. If, however, you present arguments against those reasons, as Haidt did (for example, the brother and sister used two forms of contraception, and neither was emotionally affected), they eventually get to a place of "moral dumbfounding," saying something like, "I can't explain why it's wrong, I just know it is."

Plus, brain research on moral calls of "fair" or "foul" shows that our responses often arise too quickly for them to have arrived through the slower brain process of higher-level reasoning.

There's a growing area of study in the area of "moral emotions." This view has been gaining ground for a number of years with evidence that moral judgments come from faster, more automatic emotional responses that originate outside of our skulls, in our body's reactions—as you've learned, reactions from "down low" are faster than our reasoning "up high." Researchers such as Haidt talk about how our emotions make our moral decisions and then, after that feeling has registered, our higher-level brain tries to come up with the justification.

So moral judgments are really "gut feelings"?

Researchers and writers in this area of investigation refer to certain moral emotions. Haidt has described four families of moral emotions:

- **Other-condemning:** Contempt, anger, and disgust
- **Self-conscious:** Shame, embarrassment, and guilt
- **Other-suffering:** Compassion
- **Other-praising:** Gratitude and elevation

Let's take a look at these: Anger and disgust, as many neuroscientists will tell you, are emotions that arise first in the subcortical regions, before higher-level thinking becomes involved.

And gratitude and compassion require the higher-level brain areas to be involved, as they require more complex and even abstract thinking.

So is it "down low" or "up high" that elicits moral decisions?

Moral Choices and the Brain

As is often the case, the answer appears to be *both*.

There's certainly plenty of evidence that the prefrontal cortex is involved in moral decisions—judgment and decision making need a functioning prefrontal cortex. When the prefrontal cortex is damaged, you see impulsive behavior, difficulties with decision making, decreased awareness of future consequences, and a lack of insight about how one's actions might affect someone else.

But the prefrontal cortex alone doesn't make all the calls. Subcortical parts are strongly implicated as well, including your old buddies the amygdala and the insula.

And the results of more and more studies are showing that different types of moral decisions (for example, when you're considering a personal moral dilemma versus an impersonal moral dilemma) involve different weighting of the brain areas used—amygdala, prefrontal cortex, and other variations of "low" and "high"—but that neither top nor bottom is used exclusively when it comes to moral judgment.

We still have a long way to go before we sort out exactly which brain area does what—as well as what other factors are involved—in decision making that's about something larger than yourself. But, based on the evidence to date, it seems clear that your subcortical brain parts need to work in conjunction with the ones higher up in order to allow for this kind of bigger-picture, we're-all-connected decision making. So, yes, it all comes back to brain integration.

In discussing the role of the middle prefrontal cortex in morality, Daniel Siegel, MD, said, "We come to a sense of ourselves and of others, and a sense of right action and morality, through integrative circuitry in our neural core."[3]

So, if brain integration is improved by practicing mindfulness (as it seems clear that it is), does mindfulness meditation improve your "we're all in this together" point of view, feelings, and actions?

Mindfulness, I, and Thou

What I've found in my work with my patients who practice mindfulness meditation—and what has been appearing in the research and writings about mindfulness—is that their approach to the world often becomes more and more inclusive. "Others" aren't held as such separate things after all. There's a movement in the direction of what philosopher Martin Buber referred to as an *I-Thou* attitude toward the world, in which there's mutuality and reciprocity. (In contrast, Buber said, there is the stance of *I-It,* which is a standpoint of separateness and detachment.[4] Not what we've been aiming for here!) As this shift happens, emotions and actions are more often informed by what is in service to a broader good, not just the individual or people in his or her immediate circle.

Daniel Siegel's work often refers to this phenomenon, as does that of Daniel Goleman. Looking at the studies and writings of mindfulness experts Jon Kabat-Zinn, and Richard Davidson, it's pretty clear that their findings support the notion that an "I-Thou" way of being is a reliable effect of mindfulness.

I've seen it in my psychotherapy practice: When people practice mindfulness, after a relatively short time their perceptions of their place in the world begin to shift—something corroborated by their family members. They become more broadly compassionate and more likely to act on their highest principles.

It's like having a healthier relationship with your whole global community, not just the people closest to you. When you see the world through this interconnected lens, your decisions, choices, behaviors, and relationships shift in noticeable ways.

Psychologist Louis Cozolino, eloquently frames the notion of interconnectedness in a neurological context—the "social synapse":

> Individual neurons are separated by small gaps called *synapses*. . . . [S]ynaptic transmission . . . stimulates each neuron to survive, grow, and be sculpted by experience. . . . [T]he activity within synapses is just as important as what takes place within the neurons themselves. . . .

And:

> . . . the social synapse is the space between us. It is also the medium through which we are linked together into larger organisms such as families, tribes, societies, and the human species as a whole.[5]

More Thoughts about Mindfulness and Interconnectedness

Some people get a little uncomfortable with this notion of broader belonging. Erik Erikson wrote quite a lot about the struggle between intimacy and isolation, and he talked about "distantiation," which he defined as "the readiness to repudiate, isolate, and, if necessary, destroy those forces and people whose essence seems dangerous to one's own." Erikson goes on to state,

> The lasting consequence of the need for distantiation is the readiness to fortify one's territory of intimacy and solidarity and to view all outsiders with a fanatic "overvaluation of small differences" between the familiar and the foreign. Such prejudices can be utilized and exploited in politics and in war . . .[6]

I hope you'll find the following ideas helpful as you form your own thoughts about this shift toward higher-level belonging that seems to accompany mindfulness and benefits our relationships.

- **The ethical pause.** As you learned earlier, mindfulness allows your nervous system to take the slightly longer route, which affords you that moment to make a more conscious choice in how to react or behave. It is a moment of reflecting on the results of what we do before we do it. *Will this action take me in the direction I want to go?* This is one of the essential ingredients in making "we" rather than "me" choices. (Of course, you could use your very smart prefrontal cortex to rationalize making a self-centered choice, but read on.)

- **Interdependence and connection as an act of bravery.** I've found, as Ronald Siegel, PsyD, has, the irony that "many people are drawn to meditation with the hope of becoming *invulnerable*—no longer feeling needy, insecure, or dependent on others. But it doesn't work out that way. Instead, mindfulness practice teaches us how to be vulnerable. . . . This . . . allows us to really connect with one another. Peeling off our protective layers allows us to touch and be touched. . . . Mindfulness helps us become more resilient at the same time as it makes us more vulnerable and sensitive."[7]

I consider making that choice, to really connect, to be an act of bravery, given how so many of us have erroneously come to see complete independence as the Holy Grail. (John Wayne, anyone?)

- **Scratching out social Darwinism.** The notion of "social Darwinism" is that life is all about competition, kill or be killed—and that we, as humans, have managed only by our intellect to lay down "a thin veneer hiding an otherwise selfish and brutal nature."[8]

  Except . . . consider the extensive evidence pointed out by Frans de Waal that there's a long line of animals evolutionarily "below" us on the family tree that live in cooperation, within connected, interdependent communities. They take care of the injured or weak, and they show reciprocity in their daily lives. They'll even put themselves in danger in order to protect one another. That's not just kill or be killed.

  Part of our evolutionary progress is that we actually do possess brains that aren't simply nasty and brutish underneath a veneer of cooperation. Rather, our brains actually have the wiring to operate in service to the greater good, and not just "I, me, mine." The challenge in the rapid growth of our global community is for our brains to catch up with just how large our group of kin actually is. Another piece of this challenge is for those in positions of influence to stop cultivating fear and threat as a means to get people to huddle into "us versus them" thinking in order to, oh, say, advance one's political agenda. When our fear circuitry gets activated, we regress, and mutually beneficial cooperation goes out the window.

The Big Shift

As with many of the patients I see, Justine needed to develop a greater sense of what was going on in her internal world. She had been practicing "disconnection" from herself on an hourly basis for much of her adult life.

And this had allowed her to be disconnected from the rest of the world as well.

Many of the people I see have a hard time letting go of this kind of "island" status and seeing the interconnectedness—and vulnerability—that's needed to have a relationship.

But in order to be in relationship with another, you need to remember that while you and the other exist each as your own being, you're also connected—healthily interdependent. On the same power grid.

Justine was having a hard time with the feelings that came up when she sat with the idea of how her actions impacted so many others—and how it was interfering with her connection to herself, her core values, and her own sense of right and wrong.

I helped Justine recognize the importance of her small, hour-by-hour transactions by introducing her to many of the ideas you've been learning about here:

- What wires together, fires together.
- Our daily experiences and actions change our neural connections, change our thoughts, and change how we relate to ourselves and others.
- If, like a neuron in the brain, you're consistently "firing" a message of fear-based selfishness, you're more likely to grow toward and invite connections with "selfish-firing" others, and you'll contribute to making

that the social norm not just for your own circle, but well beyond it.

Justine said that the implication made her furious. She launched into an angry tirade about how I was holding her responsible for the rise and fall of civilization and how ridiculously unfair that was and how out of touch I was with the reality of how the world worked.

I didn't get mad back, which seemed to surprise her. After a while, she was able to reconnect. I asked her to entertain another notion for just 30 seconds: if anger arises in our brains from the experience of fear, what fears might be behind her anger?

"I'm not scared of what you said. I just disagree with it. Vehemently."

She paused. There was tremendous courage in the pause. Then she went on. "Well, if that bullsh*t were true, then my whole life would have to be torn down. I'd have to leave my job, lose my house, and I'd end up like my family, scratching in the dirt for a living."

"Because . . ."

"Because if it's true, it would mean I'd have to stop doing what I do—that I'm not being a decent person, and I'll never find a decent guy if I keep doing what I'm doing. Like I'm . . . repelling them, and making the world a crappier place to boot."

She paused again. Her eyes looked ever so slightly tearful. She tried setting her jaw, adjusting her lawyerly eyeglasses, and tugging her jacket into compliance—but a tear escaped anyway.

"Okay. Now *that's* scary. I have to change everything in my life and quit my job in order to have any hope of dating someone who isn't a complete a**hole. And save the world."

We sat for a few minutes, quiet.

"So what the hell do I do now?"

Her BlackBerry buzzed.

She looked at it for a moment.

Then, for the first time in our sessions, she turned it off.

In subsequent sessions, Justine talked about how frustrated—how powerless—and how afraid she felt.

About how deep down, she felt like "a turd sandwich"—power and a beautiful home and intelligence on the outside, but morally bankrupt on the inside.

She was scared to sit with these feelings for very long, but over time she realized that she could have the feelings and not be overwhelmed by them.

She began to practice the basic mindfulness meditation, at first only in the office with me, then little by little in her daily life.

Once she "had the hang of it" a bit, I introduced Justine to the meditation exercise at the end of this chapter—on the face of it, it's just an exercise in mindful eating, but in reality, it's a primordial lesson on how we are all connected. Being mindful helps us to remember that and to make choices that are, to use one word, *moral.*

Eventually, Justine had more room and resilience to deal with the feelings that had blocked her from making changes in her life. She was able to do the hard work of figuring out what she really wanted to create with her life and who she wanted to be in the world.

She joined an urban community garden in a nearby neighborhood. She knew plenty about growing vegetables, having grown up on a farm, and enjoyed not only getting her hands in the dirt again, but also connecting with people outside of the halls of the Senate.

One of her fellow gardeners mentioned a group that was working with the urban poor to help fight hunger, getting school-age kids involved in growing vegetables for their families. Justine got in touch with the group and helped them make important connections with legislators. For her, it was easy; for the organization, it was radically helpful.

Shortly after, Justine started doing some pro bono lobbying for a group that helped farmers in the Amazon rainforest move away from clearing timber and toward non-timber forest products—providing them with an incentive to conserve the rainforest.

She did some serious soul-searching, as well as financial reprioritizing, and within six months decided to leave her lobbying firm and go to work for an environmental nonprofit group—a group to which she had been making charitable donations for years.

And, through new friends she'd made along the way, Justine met Ray. Not a Lying Liar; not a Wimpy Boy. A solid, decent guy.

INTERCONNECTEDNESS MEDITATION

I've talked a lot throughout this book about integrating your brain, getting all the parts to cooperate in service to your well-being.

Our global community similarly depends on an integration of its parts to thrive.

Buddhist monk and peace activist Thich Nhat Hanh wrote,

> A person who practices mindfulness can see things in [a] tangerine that others are unable to see. An aware person can see the tangerine tree, the tangerine blossom in the spring, the sunlight and rain which nourished the tangerine. Looking deeply, one can see ten thousand things which have made the tangerine possible . . . can see all the wonders of the universe and how all things interact with one another.[9]

If thinking about a tangerine doesn't do it for you, consider Einstein's take on it:

> A human being is a part of the whole, called by us "Universe," a part limited in time and space. He experiences himself, his thoughts and feelings as something separated from the rest—a kind of optical delusion of his consciousness. This delusion is a kind of prison for us, restricting us to our personal desires and to affection for a few persons nearest to us. Our task must be to free ourselves from this prison by widening our circle of compassion to embrace all living creatures and the whole of nature in its beauty. Nobody is able to achieve this completely, but the striving for such achievement is in itself a part of the liberation and a foundation for inner security.[10]

I invite you to try the meditation below when you can spend a little quality time with an apple. You can use a real one, or you can imagine one as you go through the exercise. You might find it helpful to start with the Basic Mindfulness Meditation Instructions at the end of Chapter 3 before moving into the meditation below.

First, take a close look at your apple. Hold it in front of you and take a few moments to see it fully. What color is it? Is there just one color, or are there many? Is it shiny all over or dull in places? Take a close look at where the stem emerges, and at the other end, where the blossom once was.

Looking at that place where the apple once was delicate petal and pollen—gone now in service to its becoming the fruit you now hold—take a moment to imagine your apple on its tree as a blossom, one among many. In your mind's eye, see the sun and the rain that helped it move from bud into flower, the bee that pollinated it to allow it to become the colorful, firm fruit in your hand. Take in a deep breath and imagine smelling the earth that held your apple's tree.

Allow yourself to imagine the farmer and farmhands who tended your apple, determined its ripeness, picked it; the driver who loaded it onto the truck, and everyone else who was a part of delivering your apple to your grocery store, setting it out on display. See if you can recall selecting it, putting it in your basket.

Take a bite of your apple and start chewing it. It's in your mouth now. Ask yourself: *Is this apple a part of me now?* (There's no right answer—just, well, food for thought.)

What about the rainwater that helped fill your apple with juiciness, the sun that its tree used to fuel its growth? Are those a part of you as you chew your apple?

After you swallow, and it's well within your belly, ask again: *Is this apple a part of me, now?*

As your apple gets broken down by your body, teased apart into nutrients that are taken up by your body—through your digestive system, into your bloodstream, into your cells, converted into energy that fuel your thoughts, feelings, and activities . . . is this apple a part of you, now?

How about the rainwater, the sun's rays, the bees, the farmer, the truck driver, the grocery-store worker? Part of you, now?

Where do you begin, what is you, and where do you end?

PART III

You've Got the POWER

CHAPTER 10

Living with Your New Wiring

When my husband and I moved into the house we currently live in, we needed to take on some minor renovations. With each project, we discovered some, er, "interesting" work that had been done by previous owners.

For example, we needed to update one of the outlets on a narrow bit of wall in the living room. When we removed a panel of beautifully crafted wood from the brick wall that lay underneath, we discovered not one, not two, but *eight* junction boxes (those rectangular metal boxes where electrical circuits come together and then branch out).

The stunning thing was that they were just . . . there. Mounted on the wall. Eight of them, no wires going in, no wires coming out.

That would be *un*integrated.

By now, you've gotten clear that having a brain that is integrated works a whole lot better than, say, a bunch of junction boxes that go nowhere.

Once you've gotten yourself on a different path—one with greater mindfulness and increased brain integration—you'll discover that the scenery along this path is different. Maybe there are new obstacles and new challenges. Maybe there are old, mystifying junction boxes revealed that were previously hidden in the walls. In this chapter, I'll provide you with some insights and leads about some of the more common scenery, discoveries, and obstacles that you might encounter.

Keep in mind that there are thousands of years of writings and teachings about what to do to begin and maintain a meditation practice, what to do when you encounter difficulties, and so on. I wouldn't dare attempt to distill all of that into one chapter. More simply, I hope to provide you with some reassurance, and in that way some company, on your journey. Company—community—holds us and helps heal us.

Common Obstacles When Rewiring Your Brain for Love

I've yet to meet anyone, myself included, who hasn't had at least a little trepidation when it comes to practicing meditation or becoming more mindful. We'll focus here on some of the thoughts and feelings that many people have about practicing mindfulness specifically in the context of better relationships.

First and Foremost

Here's the single most important idea in this chapter, the biggest thing that holds all of us back from making changes: all of us carry around self-limiting thoughts as a way of protecting ourselves from change.

And yet your thoughts, all of our thoughts, are wispy, incredibly brief neurological events, the minute spitting of neurochemicals between almost invisible cells.

They're not "the truth." They're not who you are. They're not who you always have to be.

For Better or for Worse

There's a certain safety in staying wired in the same relationship pattern that's been with you all these years. There may be unhappiness and loneliness, but at least it's an unhappiness and loneliness you know. "Better the Devil you know than the Devil you don't" is an idea going back centuries, after all. Humans don't like change much. The unknown tends to evoke fear and get our alarm systems all fired up, and change is all about the unknown. So what types of fear might you encounter on your journey?

The first is fear that things might change for the worse. This is a very logical fear. You worry that your mindfulness practice will actually be a detriment when it comes to relationships. "None of my friends will want to hang around with me if I change" is one I hear sometimes.

Or "Why look inside and stir up all of my old wounds? That'll just make me more unhappy and unlovable"—that one, and its many variations, is very popular.

The other commonly experienced, but less commonly discussed, fear is that things might change for the better, that your life might improve. "Fear of success" is not some kind of cruel joke—many of us harbor a fear of what it would mean to pursue our deepest desire.

Some people believe that they'll have to "pay" for having a healthy, loving relationship in some way, in a sort of "checks and balances" philosophy. I had a roommate in college whose childhood dog died. Her boyfriend at the time was utterly unsympathetic, saying, "That's what you get for having a dog. You get all attached, and then it dies." Woof!

There might be a lot of history telling you that you don't deserve the kind of relationship that you want; that if you get "good stuff," someone else is going to try to take it away from you or get mad enough to try to hurt you.

You might find yourself getting tangled in any or all of these—or a thousand other thoughts and worries that keep you from making the shift. (*Thoughts* again! See "First and Foremost," on page 164.)

When you bump up against these kinds of objections to practice, I find that it's often helpful to remember two things:

First, if you're walking from, say, California to New York, you're not going to get there in five minutes, or even five days. Change is a gradual process, and it's your walk, your journey. You can stop somewhere for a while to rest, to get your bearings. You can change your destination. You can decide that you like it in Montana and forget all about New York.

Second, you might indeed arrive in a different place, but try to remember that *you'll* also be different. You won't be living in the new place with your old mind-set—your integration, resilience, awareness, and other capabilities will also have changed en route.

From where your brain is now, the idea of being more present, open, and available emotionally—to yourself, to others—might be assessed as scary, undesirable, or unattainable. Rewiring the house you've lived in your whole life may seem like too massive or dangerous a task. As you move through the process, though, one step at a time, one mindfulness practice at a time, you'll be picking up new skills and tools for the job along the way. (Kind of like a video game where you acquire tools in one level for a challenge you'll face in the next.)

Another note that in itself could (and does) fill many books all by itself: somewhere in here, for many people, is confusion about who's in charge of creating your life. It's a huge responsibility to decide that you're in charge, that it's your responsibility to change things and deal with what comes up—and it's also very empowering. Sometimes owning all of that power is a little daunting, and so we give it away or try our best to dissipate it . . .

Your Partner's Resistance to Your Practice

If you're currently in a relationship and you're pursuing growth in how you "do" your relationship, there's a good likelihood that your partner may throw a few obstacles in your path—consciously or otherwise.

It might look like he or she is having a reaction to your actual meditation practice—one patient, Eva, told me that every time she went into the room where she meditated, her husband, David, would find some way to interrupt her. At first he said it was inconvenient to have her check out every day (for ten minutes).

When Eva kept practicing anyway, David started putting meditation down as "woo-woo nonsense," forwarding articles to her about the dangers of cults, and so on.

When they finally got down to the truth of the matter, David confessed that he was afraid that by meditating, Eva would figure out that he wasn't really enough for her, and she would leave him.

Rather than getting caught up in the struggle, or in David's fear, Eva approached the problem with more awareness and compassion than she'd been able to previously, and their relationship deepened for the first time in years.

This is actually one of the great potentials in your own practice: when you've been working on your own wiring, increasing your attunement, decreasing your fear, creating room for connection through your smart vagus, and so on, you're increasing the chances that your partner's brain will benefit from this work, too. (Kind of a "trickle-down" theory of brain rewiring.) What we experience the most is what our brains develop the best pathways for. So, if your partner starts to have more experience of your healthier emotional regulation, plus your increased empathy, your more attuned communication, and all of the other high-voltage relationship benefits—well, then, your partner's experience of all that can help rewire his or her brain. There can be a kind of synergy supporting growth and change.

But it doesn't always go that way. Sometimes partners are so resistant to changing how they do relationships that your growth does, indeed, lead to your decision to leave. Harriet Lerner, PhD, wrote in *The Dance of Anger,* "We cannot make another person change his or her steps to an old dance, but if we change our own steps, the dance no longer can continue in the same predictable pattern."[1]

Opening Up a Tangled Nest of Wires?

In the first house we lived in, my husband and I had quite a time with our phone service—interference on the line, losing the dial tone, and so on. The phone company's technician was up in the attic when we heard him say, "Whoa! I've been doing this for 20 years, and I have never seen anything like this!"

In a remote corner of the attic was a large metal box, easily three feet tall and two feet across. Inside, there was a tangle of multicolored wires crammed in, nearly filling the entire box. The house had apparently been wired decades before with several dozen phone lines, plus an elaborate (albeit now primitive) alarm system. The technician's best guess: "Must've been a bookie joint!"

When you're thinking about starting, restarting, or continuing a mindfulness meditation practice, you're of course going to be wondering about what nest of wiring tangles *you* might encounter.

Mindfulness may be simple, but it isn't easy. Encountering yourself with greater awareness and more honesty can be a rough ride at times. So can being more open and present with others. Being still with our own thoughts and feelings tends to make us anxious, and so we tell ourselves that we can't meditate.

Jack Kornfield, PhD, one of the pioneers in bringing mindfulness meditation to the United States and one of my favorite meditation teachers (he's also a psychologist), sums it up pretty well. He said, "There's a sign in a casino in Las Vegas that a friend of mine took and now has in his therapy room, that says, 'You must be present to win.'"[2]

Consider this, too, when you start to feel a little edgy or anxious about (or during) mindfulness practice: A pioneer of stress research, Hans Selye, MD, talked about *eustress*—good stress—as quite different from *distress*—bad stress.[3] We experience eustress when we're excited about something, or curious, or experiencing pleasure. Mild to moderate stress stimulates the release of neural growth hormones, helping your rewiring efforts. So it's actually good for you, for your brain, and for your relationships to have a little stress while you practice mindfulness.

You might even find that your tennis game improves, that you lose weight with which you've struggled for years, that you sleep better, or that you suffer less from physical ailments.

Less Drama Can Feel . . . Unsettling

In many couples, or for many singles as they date, there's a constant tumult of ups and downs, slings and arrows. When you begin to practice mindfulness, some of this drama decreases. That, on the surface, certainly sounds like a good thing. If you've become accustomed to this kind of roller-coaster drama, though, this can actually be a little unsettling—to you and to your partner. You might even feel as if, now that you have reduced your taste for drama, life is boring. It's a bit like the person struggling with recovery from addiction. Even if it's perfectly fine with you, your partner might find the relative calm unnerving—as if you've changed the rules mid-game.

Again, maintaining a mindful approach to these shifts and reactions may not only help solve the "problem" that's been created, but make it easier to get some traction on the underlying issues as well.

You Want It *When?*

When we get a little mindfulness practice under our belts, and our partners start experiencing the benefits—we're less reactive, more resilient, and so forth—they may start to like it. In fact, they may like it so much that they expect us to take everything in stride, to never "lose it" the way we used to, and to be better attuned to them in every discussion. Depending on how things had been going in your relationship before your increased brain integration, your partner may feel like it's finally a long overdue spring after a difficult winter. Invite him or her, along with your own internal critic, to be patient—empathic, even. It takes time, and no one ever *arrives* at perfectly consistent integrated mindfulness. It's an intention, not perfection. Remember: practice makes *progress.*

Turning Straw into Gold

Okay, you're getting your mindfulness groove on, you're more present and attuned and resilient and ready to be in the here and now.

And then you screw up. Or your partner brings up one of your screw-ups from the bad old days.

Doesn't feel good, but it's a gift. Really. One of the toughest things many of us struggle with is what to do with our past screw-ups—the times when we've hurt others.

You have a multitude of choices, of course. You could beat yourself up, cast the blame elsewhere, stonewall it, or ignore it.

But all those choices keep your old wiring fresh and growing, taking up valuable real estate in your brain.

Here's where screwing up can become a gift: you could, from a mindful, integrated place, own it—with empathy for your partner as well as for yourself.

Having seen the shift to this "taking ownership" in individuals and couples, I can say that it may be the single most healing and reparative thing you can do. Daniel Siegel, MD, and Mary Hartzell, MEd, write beautifully about this in the context of how we parent our kids[4]—even the most attuned, contingently responsive parents will miss the cues and signals from their children sometimes.

(By the way, being tuned in to your child 100 percent of the time would be unhealthily invasive, actually—always in your kid's head. The same is true of adult-to-adult relationships.)

Just as Siegel and Hartzell invite parents to do with their children, I invite you to think of these "oops" moments as a chance to *repair* not only the relationship, but also your old wiring, and possibly even your partner's. By doing that—by acknowledging your inevitable disconnections and misfirings (and even sparks and fires)—you and your partner start to lay down new wiring that allows for healing reconnection.

The inevitable screw-up becomes the opportunity for something vital and new in your brain, and in your relationships.

Keep Your Eyes on Your Own Mat

Comparing your mindfulness, your meditation practice, and so on to others—and/or comparing others to yourself—can lead to some pretty gnarly problems.

In one direction, you'll find yourself coming up short and being critical of yourself in unproductive ways. Since so many of us already have problems with our nasty inner critics—and with self-compassion—this is really just a path that reinforces your old patterns, maintaining your old brain wiring. Jack Kornfield has been teaching meditation in the West for decades, to thousands of people, and he has said that "half of the work people do in meditation in the West is the work of self-acceptance."[5]

And in the other direction, you might find yourself feeling a bit full of yourself. The practice of mindfulness can feel so helpful, and you can start to see things with such a different level of clarity, that you wish everyone would do it! Maybe especially your partner! And the sooner the better! ("What's the magic word?" "NOW!") If this doesn't happen, it can lead to a rift—the very gulf of indifference, abandonment, contempt, et cetera, that might have been one of the roots of relationship trouble to begin with.

A patient who studied yoga once shared with me that one of the hardest things for her about being mindful during yoga was looking around to see how she was doing compared to everyone else. "My teacher told me that the most important *asana* (yoga pose) for me was the one called 'keeping your eyes on your own mat.'"

That's excellent advice when it comes to practicing mindfulness meditation—keep your eyes on your own mat, and let your brain's increasing integration take hold for a while, like a new plant in your garden, before you start sharing cuttings of it with others.

New Company

In traditional teachings about meditation, there are many references to the "Three Jewels." Sometimes likened to the three legs of a stool, the Three Jewels can be loosely defined as safe harbors or guideposts supporting your movement toward greater mindfulness. One can be thought of as maintaining your recognition of and trust in the tremendous potential that exists within all beings. Second is the wisdom and teachings of those who have preceded you on your path toward that potential.

And the third is community. Being with others who are also committed to moving toward greater mindfulness, and with whom you can talk about and practice meditation—your "sitting buddies"—is tremendously sustaining.

Many of the patients in my practice who have tried meditation previously and found it too difficult come to realize—after finding a group of others to "sit" with—that this was the missing element for them in being able to maintain their commitment and their practice.

As a result of finding and being with others to support your practice, how you choose to spend your time and the people with whom you spend it may shift in ways that tug at the familiar or long-entrenched walls of your relationship with your partner—as well as with yourself (for example, if you've always avoided groups or identify with being a homebody).

Your partner may have some feelings about this—jealousy, anxiety, sadness, or a sense of loss. The very act of talking about this openly, and of dealing with the shift, can offer you and your relationship a breath of fresh air. That said, sometimes fresh air can be a little overwhelming when you're used to living stale.

I encourage patients who encounter these kinds of shifts in themselves (and reactions from their partners) to see them as opportunities to mindfully practice balance (for example, you don't need to abandon everything else in your life to go to group sits every spare moment), as well as set appropriate boundaries with their partners—using their burgeoning capacity for attuned communication, empathy, and so on, and without giving up their own needs.

Ups and Downs in Bed

Living with your newfound mindfulness—and all the shifting ways in which you do your relationships—can, as we discussed earlier, have some wonderful benefits for your sex life. It also means change in how you experience sex and how you experience your sexual partner.

This can reveal some of the rockier parts of the sexual terrain, including what hasn't been happening between you and your partner. As you become aware of how much vitality you feel now that you're more attuned to your own emotional and physical sensations, you might become aware, for example, of just how tuned out your partner is.

And he or she might not even understand what you're talking about: "I want you to be present when we have sex."

"What're you talking about? I'm right here!"

As with many of the challenges on this path, the most helpful approach is to see dealing with this shift in your sexual life as another place where you can exercise your new wiring pathways as you and your partner talk about the issue and explore it together. My experience is that if you can hold on to your growing capacity for attuned communication and share with your partner some of the increased pleasure that greater mindfulness brings, you'll find your way to not only better sexual intimacy, but increased connection and intimacy in other areas of your relationship as well.

All of Us Need Help from Time to Time

Sitting with your feelings, with your inner experience, and rewiring your brain and your life when it comes to love and relationships—this is Big Stuff. There may be times when you realize you're dealing with something that feels too big or too fear-provoking and decide that you may need some help.

What you're doing in mindfulness is opening up an integrated awareness of what's going on inside you—and you may be bumping up against walls that, while they no longer serve you, have been a sort of safe barrier between you and—well, between you and your self.

Sometimes, those walls are like invisible force fields—you're walking along and *bam!* You slam into it, then wonder what it was that just hit you. Getting help from an experienced psychotherapist can help you spot those walls and choose—mindfully—what to do about them.

In all likelihood, those walls were built to protect you from messages you got in your earliest attachments that your self was something bad, unlovable, and unworthy. Approaching those walls, with body regulation, emotional resilience, attunement, response flexibility, empathy, and so on, is incredibly helpful and can serve you in tremendous ways in psychotherapy.

All of us need help from time to time to see ourselves more clearly, and doing it in the presence of a psychotherapist with whom you feel connected can be invaluable. While having a psychotherapist who practices and supports mindfulness meditation can be helpful, the research on psychotherapy outcomes show that the most healing factor in psychotherapy is the therapeutic relationship—a safely boundaried connection with trust, empathy, and what is referred to as "congruence" (authenticity and genuineness from the therapist).

So, the most effective psychotherapy takes place when the therapist can be consistent and attuned; has enough self-awareness and insight to be genuine and authentic; and collaboratively responds to you in a way that's contingent on your experience and who you are.

Sound familiar? It's where we started, both in this book and in our earliest development: how a primary caregiver relates to you can profoundly affect your well-being.

Good psychotherapy, like any healthy relationship, helps move you toward improved well-being—and, I'll wager, improved brain integration, although that hasn't yet been adequately studied—by providing a place for your brain to rewire, to meet the conditions necessary for you to develop the pathways for healthy attachment. There is some research showing that areas of the brain that we believe may contribute to problems such as depression and obsessive-compulsive disorder (an anxiety disorder) change in correlation with successful psychotherapy, but we're still in the early stages of understanding this.

Finding a good psychotherapist who is right for you can be challenging. In the Resources section, you'll find some helpful information, sources, and websites to help guide you in your choice.

ABIDING CHANGES MEDITATION

Below is Ronald Siegel's "Mountain Meditation,"[6] a beautiful version of one of the first meditations I ever learned. I've turned to this meditation many times, especially while writing this book, to ground me as I experienced the shifts of challenge and change. I hope, as you continue to summon the courage to change, that you'll find it helpful too.

In this exercise you will imagine being a mountain going through seasonal changes. The first time you try this, it may work best to read about a season and then put aside the book and sit with its images for a few minutes. Once you feel you've settled into and explored one season, open your eyes briefly to read the next one and then close them again to explore it. (And, as with all of the meditations, you may want to start with the Basic Mindfulness Meditation Instructions at the end of Chapter 3.)

Spring

Imagine that you are a mountain. You're very large and very solid, and you've been on your spot for a long, long time. Of course, like all things, you change; but you change very slowly, in geologic time. At this moment it's springtime. There is life everywhere. The trees all have new leaves, flowers are in bloom, and insects are flying about. Animals are taking care of their young, the birds are back from their migrations. Each day is different—sometimes it's cloudy, cool, and raining; other times it's sunny and warm. As night turns to day and day to night, you sit there, experiencing life unfolding everywhere. As the days go by, they gradually get longer and the nights become shorter. Each one is different. You remain solid and still, experiencing all the changes on and about you.

(Close your eyes for a few minutes now and see how it feels to be a mountain in the spring, noticing all the activity on and about you.)

Summer

The days are continuing to get longer, and now it stays light until quite late. Sometimes it is quite warm, and the animals seek shade. Insects are now everywhere, crawling and flying about. Young animals are venturing out on their own. Sometimes the air is quite still and the sun is bright. Other times violent thunderstorms rumble through, lightning strikes, and rain falls in buckets. Sometimes the streams gush and tumble down your sides; other times they are nearly dry. All this activity unfolds while you sit there, quite solid, observing it all. As the days go by you notice that they are gradually becoming shorter, though they remain quite warm. You remain massive and stable, taking it all in.

(Close your eyes for a few minutes now to experience the summer.)

Autumn

The sun is now setting noticeably earlier, and the nights are beginning to be cool. You see that leaves are starting to change color and animals are preparing for winter. Birds are starting to leave. Every day is different—some are sunny and warm, but now some are cool and crisp. As day turns to night, and night to day, the leaves continue to change—some becoming brilliant in color. Sometimes it rains gently, sometimes it is stormy, other times it is quiet and peaceful. The days continue to shorten until it really gets dark early, and the nights are actually cold. You notice now that many of the trees have dropped their leaves and plants have turned from green to brown. While everything on and about you transforms, you remain relatively still and unchanging.

(Close your eyes now to be with the autumn.)

Winter

The first snow has arrived. Everything is transformed. Streams are frozen; all is covered in white. You see the animals only occasionally—mostly you notice their tracks. Very few birds are around, and the insects seem to have disappeared. Some days are sunny and warmer; others are quite cold. Fierce storms come through with blinding snow and biting wind. You're able to sit solidly, fearlessly, taking it all in.

As night turns to day and day to night you notice that the days are beginning to get longer again. Some days it's actually warm enough that the snow begins to melt and streams start to flow, but other days it all freezes again. Eventually there are more warm days than cold and you begin to see bare ground. You notice the first shoots of young plants and realize that spring is almost here.

(Again close your eyes to be with the experience.)

FINAL THOUGHTS

As I've been learning, and now as you have too, mindfulness meditation has the potential to change your brain—and your relationships, and your life. It isn't, all by itself, a panacea, something that will fix everything and make it sparkle. It's a tool, one of the most effective I've encountered in my two decades as a psychologist. I encourage you to use this precious tool, and to mindfully investigate and add other tools to your relationship toolbox as you go. I very much like the saying "If the only tool you have is a hammer, every problem is a nail." And we know that not every problem is a nail.

I also hope that as you've read this book and practiced the meditations, you've come to an awareness that healthy, vibrant relationships aren't about being free from sadness or pain. I'll leave you with this idea, from Ron Siegel:

> Modern scientific research is lining up nicely with ancient wisdom to point the way to a rich and meaningful life . . . . It includes feeling the full range of our human emotions while empathizing with everyone else's. It involves experiencing everything vividly . . . Combined with our efforts to act wisely, mindfulness practice . . . can allow us to awaken to our full potential, be more useful to others, and more completely enjoy the moments that we have together here on this planet.[1]

May you know love.

RESOURCES

Included here are lists of resources for "How do I . . . ?" and "Where can I find more about . . . ?" Fortunately, resources for those interested in mindfulness meditation, good psychotherapy, mindful parenting, and learning about the brain are all becoming more abundant and easier to find. Because of this, there is also a regularly updated list of resources at *RewireYourBrainForLove.com.*

Mindfulness Meditation Resources

Mindfulness and/or Meditation Books and Recordings

There are many excellent books for learning more about mindfulness and meditation; the few included here are those that have proven to be most helpful for my patients, friends, and family. Some are classics, some are newcomers. I encourage you to try a few different authors to find those with whom you resonate the most. Some of the authors below have multiple books and/or recordings; I've only listed one for each, and I trust that if you find a "voice" that appeals to you, you'll pursue more.

- Brach, T. (2004). *Radical acceptance: Embracing your life with the heart of a Buddha.* New York: Bantam Books.

- Chödrön, P. (Author). (2007). *Don't bite the hook: Finding freedom from anger, resentment, and other destructive emotions.* [Audiobook]. Boston: Shambhala Audio.
- Kabat-Zinn, J. (2005). *Wherever you go, there you are: Mindfulness meditation in everyday life.* New York: Hyperion Books.
- Kornfield, J. (2008). *Meditation for beginners.* Louisville, CO: Sounds True, Inc.
- Salzberg, S. (2010). *Real happiness: The power of meditation: A 28-day program.* New York: Workman Publishing Company.
- Siegel, D. J. (2007). *The mindful brain: Reflection and attunement in the cultivation of well-being.* New York: W. W. Norton & Company, Inc.
- Siegel, R. D. (2010). *The mindfulness solution: Everyday practices for everyday problems.* New York: Guilford Press.

Mindfulness Websites

As a diving-in point, I've selected just a few of the many sites on the web that offer advice and information to support mindfulness practice. If you seek more information about mindfulness online, I encourage you to be a discriminating consumer of what's offered.

- Psychologist Ronald Siegel, PsyD, has produced a collection of mindfulness meditation audio downloads that I find very useful, including the "Mountain Meditation" included in Chapter 10. They are available at no cost on his Mindfulness Solution site (case sensitive): *mindfulness-solution.com/DownloadMeditations.html.*
- The Mindful Awareness Research Center at the University of California–Los Angeles has a collection of free downloadable mindfulness meditations, as well as

other information about mindfulness and the Center: *marc.ucla.edu.*

- The Center for Compassion and Altruism Research and Education at Stanford University was founded to create a community of scholars and researchers, including neuroscientists, psychologists, neuroeconomists, and philosophical and contemplative thinkers, for the study of compassion: *ccare.stanford.edu.*

Mindfulness Meditation Organizations and Practice Centers

Finding others who are practicing mindfulness meditation is an invaluable support for anyone's mindfulness practice. The form of meditation that I focus on in this book (and that has been the subject of what I find to be the most compelling neuroscience research) is mindfulness, or insight, meditation. To help you find fellow practitioners and teachers, I've listed here some of the larger communities, organizations, and practice centers that offer opportunities to deepen your practice in mindfulness meditation.

- The Center for Mindfulness in Medicine, Health Care, and Society

  umassmed.edu/cfm
  Phone: (508) 856-2656
  E-mail: mindfulness@umassmed.edu

- Insight Meditation Center of Washington

  imcw.org
  Phone: (202) 986-2922
  E-mail: meditate@imcw.org

- Insight Meditation Society

  dharma.org
  Phone: (978) 355-4378
  E-mail: rc@dharma.org

- InsightLA
  insightla.org
  Phone: (310) 774-3325
  E-mail: via the website

- Spirit Rock Meditation Center
  spiritrock.org
  Phone: (415) 488-0164
  E-mail: SRMC@spiritrock.org

Mindful Kids, Mindful Parenting

Many of my patients, becoming more aware of their own attachment experiences and their impact on their current relationships, want to learn more about how to be more mindful parents for their own children. Here are a few of the resources that have been helpful to me as a parent and to my patients:

- Kabat-Zinn, M., & Kabat-Zinn, J. (1997). *Everyday blessings: The inner work of mindful parenting.* New York: Hyperion Books.

- Siegel, D. J., & Hartzell, M. (2004). *Parenting from the inside out: How a deeper self-understanding can help you raise children who thrive.* New York: Jeremy P. Tarcher/ Penguin.

- Greenland, S. K. (2010). *The mindful child: How to help your kid manage stress and become happier, kinder, and more compassionate.* New York: Free Press.

- The Hawn Foundation's MindUP program for education: *thehawnfoundation.org/mindup.*

Psychotherapy Resources

A good psychotherapist can be a powerful member of your rewiring team (with you as the lead electrician) to help your growth toward better relationships and well-being. As with any relationship, it can take some legwork and patience to find the right fit. As you look for a psychotherapist, keep in mind the research on psychotherapy outcomes we touched on earlier: while having a psychotherapist who practices and supports mindfulness meditation can be helpful, the most healing factor is the therapeutic relationship—a connection with trust, empathy, and congruence (authenticity and genuineness from the therapist).

As far as treatment approaches, there is a vast array of choices; some forms that specifically incorporate mindfulness practice in psychotherapy are Acceptance and Commitment Therapy (ACT: *contextualpsychology.org/act*); Dialectical Behavior Therapy (DBT: *behavioraltech.org*); and Mindfulness-Based Cognitive Therapy (MBCT: *mbct.com*). There are also non-psychotherapy forms of treatment based on mindfulness, sometimes offered by licensed mental-health professionals, including Mindfulness-Based Stress Reduction (MBSR: *umassmed.edu/cfm*), considered the "granddaddy" of mindfulness-based approaches to healing in the West.

The first and best way to start looking for a good psychotherapist is to ask people you know for recommendations. This might mean friends, family, or a trusted health-care provider. More and more psychotherapists are listing their practices online, and so you might find some leads there as well. Here are some things to keep in mind as you do your search:

- **Licensing:** Be sure that the online listing you're looking at is for a licensed mental-health professional. Very few online directories verify the credentials of providers—this is your responsibility, and a very important one in your search.

- **Educational and training background:** There are different professional degrees carried by mental-health professionals, and the licensing requirements for each vary (even from state to state within the U.S.). In addition, the titles of mental-health providers mean different things in different jurisdictions. For example, use of the title *psychologist* is protected by law in most states, but the term *psychotherapist* or *counselor* might be unregulated.
- As a basic guide to the alphabet soup of academic degrees held by mental-health professionals, there are:
    - **Psychologists** (doctoral degree in psychology; PhD and PsyD are the most common designations)
    - **Clinical social workers** (master's degree in social work: MSW, LCSW, and LICSW are common designations)
    - **Psychiatrists** (medical degree: MD or DO)
    - **Psychiatric clinical nurse specialists** (CNS)
    - **Other titles:** In many states, there are master's-level practitioners (for example, MA, MFT, and MDiv) who may be licensed to provide mental health services.

There are a number of large online directories to help you in your search, such as *GoodTherapy.org,* and smaller, more specialized ones, such as *ContemplativePsychotherapy.net.* Please remember that finding someone by browsing an online directory or by using a particular search term is no guarantee that you're getting what you searched for. Entering "psychiatrist" as a search term, for example, could lead you to providers who are not, in fact, psychiatrists. Always remember that most online directories do not verify the credentials or licensure of those who are listed—that responsibility is yours.

We now know a great deal about the importance of being in the physical presence of an attuned person for healing and well-being of the "relationship brain," so I feel that online psychotherapy or psychotherapy by phone should be used only in extreme circumstances, when in-person sessions aren't possible.

Finally, mindfulness is used increasingly in psychotherapy settings, but providers who have experience with using mindfulness as part of treatment are still relatively rare. Keep in mind that whether or not the psychotherapist you choose is mindfulness-savvy, your own mindfulness practice will help your therapeutic process and progress.

Delving Deeper: Research on Mindfulness, the Brain, and Relationships

I'm grateful that there are now thousands of research articles, books, and other academic resources for the study of how the brain, mindfulness, and relationships interact and shape one another. What guides me day in and day out with my patients, and what I have written here, is drawn from hundreds of those resources. For those who may be interested in wading into the research river, the website for this book, *RewireYourBrainForLove.com,* has a more comprehensive bibliography of the books, journal articles, and other materials used in my own pursuit of understanding this field and in the writing of this book.

Staying up to date with the research is exciting, and one resource that has been extremely helpful is *Mindfulness Research Monthly,* compiled each month by David S. Black, PhD. You can find a link to these monthly updates here: *mindfulexperience.org.*

I also created *RewireYourBrainForLove.com,* where you can navigate to a full bibliographic listing for this book, as well as many resources, links, new articles I've written, videos, blog posts, and other good stuff related to mindfulness, neuroscience, and relationships. If you're interested, you can register for my monthly newsletter there, or join me on Facebook.

ENDNOTES

Introduction

1. For example, Lambert, M. J., & Barley, D. E. (2001). Research summary on the therapeutic relationship and psychotherapy outcome. *Psychotherapy: Theory, Research, Practice, Training,* 38, 357–361.
2. Baime, M. (2011, July). This is your brain on mindfulness. *Shambhala Sun,* 44–48, 84.

Chapter 1

1. Cozolino, L. (2008, September/October). It's a jungle in there: We're not as evolved as we think. *Psychotherapy Networker,* 20–27.
2. There are a number of different measures of both childhood and adult attachment patterns or styles, but various studies show that (a) childhood patterns of attachment are generally quite stable throughout the lifespan in the general population (e.g., Fraley, C. [2002]. Attachment stability from infancy to adulthood: Meta-analysis and dynamic modeling of developmental mechanisms. *Personality and Social Psychology Review,* 6, 123–151) and (b) roughly 55 percent of children have secure attachment, a decrease of close to 10 percent

between 1995 and 2005 (Sroufe, L. A., Egeland, B., Carlson, E. A., & Collins, W. A. [2005]. *The development of the person: The Minnesota study of risk and adaptation from birth to adulthood.* New York: Guilford Press).

Chapter 2

1. Diamond, M.C. (1991). Hormonal effects on the development of cerebral lateralization. *Psychoneuroendocrinology,* 16, 121–129.
2. For example, Decety, J., Jackson, P. L., Sommerville, J. A., Chaminade, T., & Meltzoff, A. N. (2004). The neural bases of cooperation and competition: an fMRI investigation. *NeuroImage,* 23, 744–751.
3. Lazar, S. W., Kerr, C. E., Wasserman, R. H., Gray, J. R., Greve, D. N., Treadway, M. T., McGarvey, M., Quinn, B. T., Dusek, J. A., Benson, H., Rauch, S. L., Moore, C. I., & Fischl, B. (2005). Meditation experience is associated with increased cortical thickness. *Neuroreport,* 16(17), 1893–1897.

4 Allman, J. M., Tetreault, N. A., Hakeem, A. Y., Manaye, K. F., Semendeferi, K., Erwin, J. M., Park, S., Goubert, V., & Hof, P. R. (2011). The von Economo neurons in the frontoinsular and anterior cingulate cortex. *Annals of the New York Academy of Sciences,* 1225, 59–71.

5 Heimer, L., Van Hoesen, G. W., Trimble, M., & Zahm, D. S. (2008). *Anatomy of neuropsychiatry: The new anatomy of the basal forebrain and its implications for neuropsychiatric illness.* Burlington, MA: Academic Press.

Chapter 3

1. Steven Porges writes and lectures extensively about his polyvagal theory; one source for more information is his 2011 book *The Polyvagal Theory: Neurophysiological Foundations of Emotions, Attachment, Communication, and Self-regulation.* New York: W. W. Norton.

2. I asked Steven Porges about why he switched from the old-school *branches* to using the term *circuits*. His response: "I use the term *circuit* to emphasize the bidirectional feedback between periphery organs and brain stem areas. Branches focus on the 'efferent' pathways or outputs to the periphery." In more colloquial terms, he made the change because he wanted to convey the "round-trip" aspect of information flow.
3. Ortigue, S., Grafton, S. T., & Bianchi-Demicheli, F. (2007). Correlation between insula activation and self-reported quality of orgasm in women. *NeuroImage,* 37(2), 551–560.
4. Lazar, S. W., et al. (2005). Meditation experience is associated with increased cortical thickness. (See Chapter 3, note 7.)
5. Hölzel, B. K., Ott, U., Hempel, H., Hackl, A., Wolf, K., Stark, R., & Vaitl, D. (2007). Differential engagement of anterior cingulate and adjacent medial frontal cortex in adept meditators and non-meditators. *Neuroscience Letters,* 421(1), 16–21.
6. Hölzel, B. K., Carmody, J., Vangel, M., Congleton, C., Yerramsetti, S. M., Gard, T., & Lazar, S. W. (2011). Mindfulness practice leads to increases in regional brain gray matter density. *Psychiatry Research: Neuroimaging,* 191, 36–43.
7. The original quote, attributed to 1940s movie star Rosalind Russell: "Taking joy in life is a woman's best cosmetic."

Chapter 4

1. "Tiger" metaphor adapted from Eifert, G. H., & Forsyth, J. P. (2005). *Acceptance & commitment therapy for anxiety disorders: A practitioner's treatment guide to using mindfulness, acceptance, and values-based behavior change strategies.* Oakland, CA: New Harbinger Publications.
2. Related by Heisenberg, quoted in Salam, A. (1990). *Unification of fundamental forces: The first of the 1988 Dirac Memorial Lectures.* Cambridge: Cambridge University Press.
3. Flatow, I. (Interviewer/Host), & Schlozman, S. (Interviewee). (2009, October 30). Science Friday: A head-shrinker studies the zombie brain [Interview transcript].

Retrieved from http://www.npr.org/templates/story/story.php?storyId=114319726.

4. Tang, Y. Y., Ma, Y., Wang, J., Fan, Y., Feng, S., Lu, Q., Yu, Q., Sui, D., Rothbart, M. K., Fan, M., & Posner, M. I. (2007). Short-term meditation training improves attention and self-regulation. *Proceedings of the National Academy of Sciences,* 104(43), 17152–17156.

5. Simpson, J. A. (1990). Influence of attachment styles on romantic relationships. *Journal of Personality and Social Psychology,* 59(5), 971–980.

6. Siegel, D.J. (1999). *The developing mind: How relationships and the brain interact to shape who we are* (p.117). New York: Guilford.

7. Pietromonaco, P. R., & Carnelley, K. B. (1994). Gender and working models of attachment: Consequences for perceptions of self and romantic relationships. *Personal Relationships,* 1, 63–82.

Chapter 5

1. Personal communication, March 26, 2010.

2. Personal communication, October 8, 2009.

3. Hooker, C. I., Gyurak, A., Verosky, S. C., Miyakawa, A., & Ayduk, O. (2010). Neural activity to a partner's facial expression predicts self-regulation after conflict. *Biological Psychiatry,* 67(5), 406–413.

4. Creswell, J. D., Way, B. M., Eisenberger, N. I., & Lieberman, M. D. (2007). Neural correlates of dispositional mindfulness during affect labeling. *Psychosomatic Medicine,* 69, 560–565.

5. Davidson's lab has published a number of articles on this topic; for example: Davidson, R. (1992). Emotion and affective style: Hemispheric substrates. *Psychological Science,* 3(1), 39–43; and Urry, H. L., Nitschke, J. B., Dolski, I., Jackson, D. C., Dalton, K. M., Mueller, C. J., Rosenkranz, M. A., Ryff, C. D., Singer, B. H., & Davidson, R. J. (2004). Making a life worth living: Neural correlates of well-being. *Psychological Science,* 15(6), 367–372.

Chapter 6

1. Goleman, D. (2006). *Emotional intelligence: Why it can matter more than IQ (10th Anniversary Edition).* New York: Bantam Dell.

2. Brach, T. (2004). *Radical acceptance: Embracing your life with the heart of a Buddha.* New York: Bantam Dell.

Chapter 7

1. Wylie, M. S. (2004, September/October). Mindsight: Dan Siegel offers therapists a new vision of the brain. *Psychotherapy Networker,* 29–39.

Chapter 8

1. Neal. D. T., & Chartrand, T. L. (2011). Embodied emotion perception: Amplifying and dampening facial feedback modulates emotion perception accuracy. *Social Psychological and Personality Science.* Advance online publication. doi: 10.1177/1948550611406138.

2. Carr, L., Iacoboni, M., Dubeau, M. C., Mazziotta, J. C., & Lenzi, G. L. (2003). Neural mechanisms of empathy in humans: A relay from neural systems for imitation to limbic areas. *Proceedings of the National Academy of Science,* 100, 5497–5502.

3. How could I possibly resist including a note for George Carlin? Carlin, G. (1972). *Class Clown* [Audio recording]. New York: Little David.

4. Brach, T. (2004). *Radical acceptance.* (See Chapter 6, note 2.)

5. Salzberg, S. (2002). *Lovingkindness: The Revolutionary Art of Happiness.* Boston: Shambhala Publications.

6. Salzberg, S. (2002). *Lovingkindness.*

Chapter 9

1. Kennedy, J. F. (1963, June). Commencement address at American University, Washington, D.C.

2. Haidt, J. (2001). The emotional dog and its rational tail: A social intuitionist approach to moral judgment. *Psychological Review,* 108, 814–834.

3. Siegel, D. J. (2007). *The mindful brain: Reflection and attunement in the cultivation of well-being.* New York: W. W. Norton & Company, Inc.

4. Buber, M. (1971). *I and thou* (W. Kaufmann, Trans.). New York: Touchstone. (Original work published 1923, *Ich und Du.*)

5. Cozolino, L. (2006). *The neuroscience of human relationships: Attachment and the developing social brain.* New York: W. W. Norton & Company, Inc.

6. Erikson, E. H. (1968). *Identity: Youth and crisis.* New York: W.W. Norton & Company, Inc.

7. Siegel, R. D. (2010): *The mindfulness solution: Everyday practices for everyday problems.* New York: Guilford Press.

8. de Waal, F. (2006). *Primates and philosophers: How morality evolved.* Princeton: Princeton University Press.

9. Hanh, T. N. (1991). *Old path white clouds: Walking in the footsteps of the Buddha.* Berkeley, CA: Parallax Press.

10. Sullivan, W. (1972, March 29). The Einstein papers: Man of many parts was long involved in the cause of peace. *New York Times* (1923-Current file). Retrieved from ProQuest Historical Newspapers *The New York Times* (1851–2007). (Document ID: 90712456).

Chapter 10

1. Lerner, H. (2001). *The dance of anger: A woman's guide to changing the patterns of intimate relationships.* New York: Quill.

2. Mishlove, J. (Interviewer) & Kornfield, J. (Interviewee). (Year

unknown). The practice of meditation with Jack Kornfield, PhD. In Mishlove, J., *Thinking Allowed: Conversations on the Leading Edge of Discovery.* Oakland, CA: Thinking Allowed Productions.

3. Selye, H. (1956). *The stress of life.* New York: McGraw-Hill.
4. Siegel, D. J., & Hartzell, M. (2004). *Parenting from the inside out: How a deeper self-understanding can help you raise children who thrive.* New York: Jeremy P. Tarcher/Penguin.
5. Mishlove, J. (Interviewer) & Kornfield, J. (Interviewee). (Year unknown). (See note 2.)
6. Siegel, R. D. (2010). *The mindfulness solution.* (See chapter 9, note 7.)

Final Thoughts

1. Siegel, R. D. (2010). *The mindfulness solution.* (See chapter 9, note 7.)

ACKNOWLEDGMENTS

The process that led to the writing of this book brought together some previously disconnected but deeply important threads in my life. Weaving those threads together has taken the help, love, insight, and wisdom of many.

I'm grateful to the patients who have honored me with their trust, their journeys, and their courage. It has been your hard work and commitment toward creating more love and connection in your lives that inspired me to take this project on.

I'm deeply indebted to the researchers, clinicians, teachers, and other great minds who have informed and inspired me, including Richie Davidson, Jon Kabat-Zinn, Sue Johnson, Sara Lazar, Ron Siegel, Dan Siegel, Lou Cozolino, Dan Goleman, Stephen Porges, Frans de Waal, Phil Best, Pete Brunjes, Rich Lewine, and the late Edith Kaplan and Mary Ainsworth—so many of you were incredibly generous with your time, knowledge, and sagacity in helping me dig deeper while writing this book. Honors in the warm and frank feedback category go to Lou Cozolino and Ron Siegel. You both not only helped tremendously with the book, but with my healing from some old grad-school nightmares as well.

Big thanks (and my fervent wishes for bountiful funding) to NIH and NIMH for supporting the important research on the brain, the mind, and our humanity. On a more personal note, your funding also made it possible for me to subsist on more than just ramen noodles and peanut butter on the way to my doctorate many years ago. Thanks.

My heartfelt gratitude to those who have taught me, directly and indirectly, about mindfulness, including Jack Kornfield, Tara Brach, Sharon Salzberg, Jon Kabat-Zinn, Ron Siegel, Belleruth Naparstek, Herb Benson, Thich Nhat Hanh, and, way back when I was an anxious third grader, Arnie Lazarus, whose voice, even through a cheap, banged-up portable cassette player, managed to guide me to sleep.

Thank you, thank you, thank you on so many levels to David Pellegrini, for your years of patience, warmth, laughter, and phenomenally healing attunement. Rewiring, indeed.

For keeping me company—and for "getting" me—I give huge thanks to and for my friends, most especially "The Divas" (Susan Berlin, Ellen Carr, and Tamara Lubliner) who have cheered me on and loved me despite my many imitations of a prairie dog during this project, disappearing and popping back up more times than I can count. I can only aspire to be as abiding.

The path of writing this book took me many places of unexpected joy—including finding again my wise, creative, separated-at-birth kin, Leslie Harrison (the living example of the saying that good friends are like stars: you don't always see them, but you know they're always there).

Big-time gratitude and love to my family of origin, every one of you, for the jokes as well as the challenges, the stories and the neuroses, the support and the *WTF?!* moments that have so richly contributed to my own wiring.

My literary agent, Bonnie Solow, has been steadfast in her belief in and support of me, a complete unknown to her when we started. (We'll have to make a deal—you get to clone me if I get to clone you.) Gay Hendricks's "awarding" Bonnie's attention to me was truly an extraordinary, life-changing gift. It was also a gift to have been introduced to Chris Foley of Foleypod, who brought his ingenuity, technability, and integrity to the development of my e-presence.

Before I even really knew what the heck I was trying to do, some of the earliest support and editing of what turned into this book came from the very wonderful Paul B. Brown, Jeremy Katz (now at KatzInk), and Nancy Peske.

Having a publishing team that values, responds, and supports me the way that Hay House has done is a rare and lovely experience. Patty Gift, Laura Koch, and Sally Mason in the New York office—y'all have been a dream to work with. Christy Salinas's patience and keen design eye went above and beyond. The whole team, from acquisition to launch, has earned my deep respect and thanks. More Neurochocolates for everyone!

As I've written this book, I've been fueled on a daily basis by what once never even existed: a cadre of e-subscribers, readers on my blog, followers on Twitter, fans on Facebook, and every other corner of cyberspace. It's a challenge to "e-connect" with meaning and depth, but you all have taught me much about the blessing of those whom we've never met. I hope to meet more of you IRL.

Speaking of online treasure troves, I'm also grateful to the many colleagues with whom I now have hundreds of connections, thanks to the interwebs, ranging from "basic science" researchers to practitioners and healers to those who have as garnered as much knowledge as many of the credentialed folks by self-educating yourself in this realm of well-being. I can't possibly thank all of you here, but anyone curious enough to take a peek at my Facebook and Twitter following will find many of these fantastic folks. I feel especially grateful for those mindfulness, brain, and/or relationship peeps whom I initially met "virtually," including Rick Hanson, Bonnie Badenoch, Elisha Goldstein, David Rock, Lisa Kift, Priscilla Warner, Shamash Alidina, Ed Halliwell, Susan Kaiser Greenland, and Linda Graham. I encourage you to seek out their expertise and wise writings.

While I'm neither Tibetan nor Buddhist, I am profoundly honored to thank His Holiness the 14th Dalai Lama for so many things, but especially for saying to neuroscience, "First investigate the positive effects of meditation. If you find it successful, please teach it to your society in a purely secular manner in order to benefit everyone."

Thank you to my husband, Duncan Krieger, for his steadfast "being there" through all of the ups and downs, aparts and togethers. I'm pretty sure that your previous career of running into burning buildings prepared you at least a little bit for being my partner during the birthing of this book. Being an insightful, loving person to your core certainly helped, too. I'm deeply grateful, and I love you a ton.

And last but certainly not least, thank you to my most powerful teacher, my heart on two legs, who was asked to be much too patient during this project, and who insisted that I figure out how to show up anyway: Gabriel, whom I love soooooo much, forever and ever and always.

ABOUT THE AUTHOR

Marsha Lucas, PhD, is a licensed psychologist and neuropsychologist and has been practicing psychotherapy and studying the brain-behavior relationship for nearly 20 years. Prior to entering private practice, she was a neuropsychologist on the faculty at the Emory University School of Medicine.

She fell in love with interpersonal neurobiology in a conference room full of 750 other people—finding herself getting some odd looks when she had tears of joy rolling down her face at the mention of the anterior cingulate and the insula in the same sentence as "greater empathy." She appreciates the integration of mindfulness, neuroscience, and relationships as a perfect confluence of many of the previously unintegrated aspects of her life.

Dr. Lucas maintains a clinical private practice in Washington, D.C. She lives in suburban D.C. with her husband, Duncan Krieger, their son, Gabriel, and their dog, Bodhi.

Hay House Titles of Related Interest

YOU CAN HEAL YOUR LIFE, the movie,
starring Louise L. Hay & Friends
(available as a 1-DVD program, an expanded
2-DVD set, and an online streaming video)
Learn more at: **www.LouiseHayMovie.com**

THE SHIFT, the movie,
starring Dr. Wayne W. Dyer
(available as a 1-DVD program, an expanded
2-DVD set, and an online streaming video)
Learn more at: **www.DyerMovie.com**

♡

FRIED: Why You Burn Out and How to Revive,
by Joan Borysenko, PhD

TRAVELING AT THE SPEED OF LOVE, by Sonia Choquette

WHY MEDITATE?: Working with Thoughts and Emotions,
by Matthieu Ricard

WIRED FOR JOY!: A Revolutionary Method for Creating Happiness from Within, by Laurel Mellin

♡

We hope you enjoyed this Hay House book. If you'd like to receive our online catalog featuring additional information on Hay House books and products, or if you'd like to find out more about the Hay Foundation, please contact:

HAY HOUSE

Hay House, Inc., P.O. Box 5100, Carlsbad, CA 92018-5100
(760) 431-7695 or (800) 654-5126
(760) 431-6948 (fax) or (800) 650-5115 (fax)
www.hayhouse.com® • www.hayfoundation.org

Published in Australia by: Hay House Australia Pty. Ltd., 18/36 Ralph St., Alexandria NSW 2015
Phone: 612-9669-4299 • *Fax:* 612-9669-4144
www.hayhouse.com.au

Published in the United Kingdom by: Hay House UK, Ltd., The Sixth Floor, Watson House, 54 Baker Street, London W1U 7BU
Phone: +44 (0)20 3927 7290 • *Fax:* +44 (0)20 3927 7291
www.hayhouse.co.uk

Published in India by: Hay House Publishers India, Muskaan Complex, Plot No. 3, B-2, Vasant Kunj, New Delhi 110 070
Phone: 91-11-4176-1620 • *Fax:* 91-11-4176-1630
www.hayhouse.co.in
